MY WORSHIP PLANNER AND ORGANIZER

**Three-Year Record Keeper
For Lectionary Users**

BY GLORIA M. MEURANT

C.S.S. Publishing Co., Inc.
Lima, Ohio

Library of Congress Cataloging-In-Publication Data

Meurant, Gloria M., 1921-
    My worship planner and organizer: three-year record keeper for lectionary users / by Gloria M. Meurant.
        p.   cm.
    ISBN 1-55673-439-5
    1. Public worship.   2. Church music.   3. Common Lectionary. I. Title.
BV15.M48   1992
2364'.00212—dc20   92-24046
                                                                                        CIP

9242 / ISBN 1-55673-439-5   PRINTED IN U.S.A.

To Trinity Lutheran Church at Vernon, Connecticut, and Advent Lutheran Church at Boca Raton, Florida, wherein the bodies of Christ, with loving care, have baptized, taught, confirmed, nurtured and sustained this grateful child of God for a lifetime.

Table Of Contents

Introduction

May this and all things work to the glory of the Triune God: To the Father who created and loved us, to the Son who loved and saved us, and to the Holy Spirit who loves and guides us in this life and time, wherein we have hope for life eternal.

The information herein is gathered together in the hope that it will assist all those involved in Christian Liturgy. It is with quiet joy that I serve God and, hopefully, you.

With thanks and praise to the Lord who chose to plant the idea, and provided the resources; and who, thereafter, granted me its humble completion and the courage to try to find a way to share it.

May you be blessed in its use.

Foreword

Few of God's saints this side of our heavenly home have more reason, through personal experience, to know the truth of Paul's words that we are "... always carrying in the body the death of Jesus (2 Corinthians 4:10a)." God's baptized child, Gloria Meurant, has been at death's door too many times for that not to be the case. And I've been there with her for too many of those occasions. Let me explain.

It was my precious treasure to serve as Gloria's parish pastor for four years. She served as chair of our board for worship and spiritual life and, in that position, was my ministry colleague in planning the corporate worship life of our congregation. Her approach to that is the gift she shares with you in these pages. I can attest to the value of those materials because I was blessed with the opportunity to live with them as her gift long before she ever thought of publishing them.

You should know, by the way, that Gloria never attended seminary. To my knowledge, she never took even an entry level course in liturgy. So what qualifies her to write this helpful guide for worship planning?

It's simple, from my point of view. It's not just that she's as well-read in scripture, the liturgical tradition of the Lutheran Church, the *Lutheran Book of Worship* and the many manuals and supporting books available as few pastors that I know. It's that the sacramental, liturgical, devotional and spiritual life of the church is the very lifeblood of her being.

That's why I'm glad you have the gift of this book of worship planning assistance. It shares a bit of the gift she's been for me, and so many others, over the years of her particular ministry.

Paul concludes the passage with which I began these paragraphs with these words: ". . . so that the life of Jesus may also be made visible in our bodies. For while we live, we are always being given up to death for Jesus' sake, so that the life of Jesus may be made visible in our mortal flesh (11b-12)."

I'm sure that is the only reason Gloria Meurant is offering this gift to all of us. May it help you toward that end in your life and ministry even as it has done so in a profound way in my own.

Paul O. Lutze
Tampa, Florida

First Sunday In Advent

Readings

LESSON	CYCLE A	CYCLE B	CYCLE C
	Revised Common	**Revised Common**	**Revised Common**
First	Isaiah 2:1-5	Isaiah 64:1-9	Jeremiah 33:14-16
Second	Romans 13:11-14	1 Corinthians 1:3-9	1 Thessalonians 3:9-13
Gospel	Matthew 24:36-44	Mark 13:24-37	Luke 21:25-36
	Episcopal	**Episcopal**	**Episcopal**
First	Isaiah 2:1-5	Isaiah 64:1-9a	Zechariah 14:4-9
Second	Romans 13:8-14	1 Corinthians 1:1-9	1 Thessalonians 3:9-13
Gospel	Matthew 24:37-44	Mark 13:(24-32) 33-37	Luke 21:25-31
	Lutheran	**Lutheran**	**Lutheran**
First	Isaiah 2:1-5	Isaiah 63:16b-17; 64:1-8	Jeremiah 33:14-16
Second	Romans 13:11-14	1 Corinthians 1:3-9	1 Thessalonians 3:9-13
Gospel	Matthew 24:37-44 or Matthew 21:1-11	Mark 13:33-37 or Mark 11:1-10	Luke 21:25-36
	Roman Catholic	**Roman Catholic**	**Roman Catholic**
First	Isaiah 2:1-5	Isaiah 63:16b-17; 64:1, 3b-8	Jeremiah 33:14-16
Second	Romans 13:11-14	1 Corinthians 1:3-9	1 Thessalonians 3:12—4:2
Gospel	Matthew 24:37-44	Mark 13:33-37	Luke 21:25-28, 34-36

Notes	Special Notes For A	Special Notes For B	Special Notes For C
Creed: Nicene **Color:** Blue/purple **Special Notation:** First Sunday of the church year.	Advent wreath originated in eastern Germany. At advent services, some four persons with a name derived from "John" could light candles. Candle colors might match paraments.	Gospel reading may be by solo voices during individual lines with all voices combined to say the repetitive admonition "Watch!" Saturday before 1st Sunday In Advent could be church's New Year's Eve. Might include Advent workshop, potluck meal and special music. Projects might be calendars for year with devotional material and places for local church events.	The gospel announces "last things." We are between a kingdom which has come and will come. We look forward because we look back. How would John answer soldiers and tax collectors today? When has God visited our lives?

Music For Worship For First Sunday In Advent

NOTES

CYCLE A	CYCLE B	CYCLE C
First Lesson O Savior, Rend The Heavens Wide O God Of Love, O King Of Peace O God Of Every Nation God The Omnipotent **Second Lesson** Wake, Awake, For Night Is Flying Hark, A Thrilling Voice Is Sounding! O Lord, How Shall I Meet You Come, Thou Long-Expected Jesus The King Shall Come The Lord Will Come And Not Be Slow The Day Is Surely Drawing Near Come, O Precious Ransom Prepare The Royal Highway	Wake, Awake, For The Night Is Flying The Lord Will Come And Not Be Slow O Day Full Of Grace O God, Our Help In Ages Past Greet, Now The Swiftly Changing Year Herald, Sound The Note Of Judgment My Hope Is Built On Nothing Less Lord! Enthroned in Heavenly Splendor Crown Him With Many Crowns All Hail The Power Of Jesus' Name! O Morning Star, How Fair and Bright Now All The Vault Of Heaven Resounds Alleluia! Sing To Jesus Rise, O Children Of Salvation The Son Of God Goes Forth To War	The Day Is Surely Drawing Near Oh Come, Oh Come, Emmanuel Through The Night Of Doubt And Sorrow A Stable Lamp Is Lighted

Weekly Record

Date				
Entrance Hymn				
Hymn Of The Day				
Anthem/ Special Music				
Sermon Title				
Lay Reader				
Attendance				

Second Sunday In Advent

Readings

LESSON		CYCLE A	CYCLE B	CYCLE C
		Revised Common	**Revised Common**	**Revised Common**
First		Isaiah 11:1-10	Isaiah 40:1-11	Baruch 5:1-9 or Malachi 3:1-4
Second		Romans 15:4-13	2 Peter 3:8-15a	Philippians 1:3-11
Gospel		Matthew 3:1-12	Mark 1:1-8	Luke 3:1-6
		Episcopal	**Episcopal**	**Episcopal**
First		Isaiah 11:1-10	Isaiah 40:1-11	Baruch 5:1-9
Second		Romans 15:4-13	2 Peter 3:8-15a, 18	Philippians 1:1-11
Gospel		Matthew 3:1-12	Mark 1:1-8	Luke 3:1-6
		Lutheran	**Lutheran**	**Lutheran**
First		Isaiah 11:1-10	Isaiah 40:1-11	Malachi 3:1-4
Second		Romans 15:4-13	2 Peter 3:8-14	Philippians 1:3-11
Gospel		Matthew 3:1	Mark 1:1-8	Luke 3:1-6
		Roman Catholic	**Roman Catholic**	**Roman Catholic**
First		Isaiah 11:1-10	Isaiah 4:1-5, 9-11	Baruch 5:1-9
Second		Romans 15:4-9	2 Peter 3:8-14	Philippians 1:4-6, 8-11
Gospel		Matthew 3:1-12	Mark 1:1-8	Luke 3:1-6

Notes	Special Notes For A	Special Notes For B	Special Notes For C
Creed: Nicene **Color:** Blue or purple **Special Notation:**	Lessons present Old Testament images descriptive of arrival of the Messiah. Jesse was the father of King David from whom the Messiah would be a descendant, giving him the title of "root of Jesse."	One person could read gospel narrative and another say John's parts. Banner could show someone half immersed in water in a posture of contrition.	John prepared "the way of the Lord" by proclaiming "a baptism of repentance for the forgiveness of sins. How are our roads straightened and our rough places made smooth? Relate scripture texts to our own experiences.

Music For Worship For Second Sunday Of Advent

NOTES	CYCLE A	CYCLE B	CYCLE C
	Oh Come, Oh Come, Emmanuel	Prepare The Royal Highway	(Stanza 3) Love Divine, All Love Excelling
	Cold December Flies Away	Comfort, Comfort Now My People	Prepare The Royal Highway
	Let Our Gladness Have No End	By All Your Saints In God's Mercy	Comfort, Comfort Now My People
	Lo, How A Rose Is Growing	There's A Wilderness In God's Mercy	Let Us Ever Walk With Jesus
	(first and second lesson)	When Christmas Morn Is Dawning	Oh, That I Had A Thousand Voices
	Comfort, Comfort Now My People	Son of God, Eternal Savior	
	Hark! A Thrilling Voice Is Sounding	Stand Up, Stand Up For Jesus	
		Open Now Thy Gates Of Beauty	
		Let A Mortal Flesh Keep Silence	
		All Who Believe And Are Baptized	
		A Savior Precious Savior	
		Dear Lord And Father Of Mankind	
		Lead On, O King Eternal	

Weekly Record

Date						
Entrance Hymn						
Hymn Of The Day						
Anthem/ Special Music						
Sermon Title						
Lay Reader						
Attendance						

Third Sunday In Advent

Readings

LESSON	CYCLE A	CYCLE B	CYCLE C
First Second Gospel	**Revised Common** Isaiah 35:1-10 James 5:7-10 Matthew 11:2-11	**Revised Common** Isaiah 61:1-4, 8-11 1 Thessalonians 5:16-24 John 1:6-8, 19-28	**Revised Common** Zephaniah 3:14-18a Philippians 4:4-7 Luke 3:7-18
First Second Gospel	**Episcopal** Isaiah 35:1-10 James 5:7-10 Matthew 11:2-11	**Episcopal** Isaiah 65:17-25 1 Thessalonians 5:(12-15) 16-28 John 1:6-8 or John 3:23-30	**Episcopal** Zephaniah 3:14-20 Philippians 4:4-7 (8, 9) Luke 3:7-18
First Second Gospel	**Lutheran** Isaiah 35:1-10 James 5:7-10 Matthew 11:2-11	**Lutheran** Isaiah 61:1-3, 10-11 1 Thessalonians 5:16-24 John 1:6-8, 19-28	**Lutheran** Zephaniah 3:14-18a Philippians 4:4-7 (8, 9) Luke 3:7-18
First Second Gospel	**Roman Catholic** Isaiah 35:1-6a, 10 James 5:7-10 Matthew 11:2-11	**Roman Catholic** Isaiah 61:1-2, 10-11 1 Thessalonians 5:16-24 John 1:6-8, 19-28	**Roman Catholic** Zephaniah 3:14-18a Philippians 4:4-7 Luke 3:10-18

Notes

	Special Notes For A	Special Notes For B	Special Notes For C
	The theme is the restoration of blind, deaf and disabled people to fullness of life. Here is evidence of God's messianic activity. We are urged to exercise a patient watchfulness for the coming of the Lord.	Banner: Someone pointing to an unseen figure, or figures representing the Messiah, Elijah, the prophet "like Moses" and the "forerunner."	Just as John preached "good news," the church is entrusted with this message during the period of his exaltation and before he returns. Study John's answers to: "Teacher, what shall we do?" "Grant us, your people, the wisdom to see your purpose today and the openness to hear your will, that we may witness to Christ's coming and so prepare his way."

Creed: Nicene
Color: Blue or purple
Special Notation:

Music For Worship For Third Sunday In Advent

NOTES

CYCLE A

First Lesson
The King Shall Come
Hark, The Glad Sound
Children Of The Heavenly Father
Joyful, Joyful We Adore Thee

Second Lesson
The Advent Of Our God
O Lord, How Shall I Meet You
Rejoice, Rejoice, Believers
Battle Hymn Of The Republic

Gospel
Comfort, Comfort Now My People
God, Whose Almighty Word

CYCLE B

Hark, The Glad Sound
The Only Son From Heaven
By All Your Saints In Welfare
Battle Hymn Of The Republic
Ye Watchers And Ye Holy Ones
God Himself Is Present
God Has Spoken By His Prophets
In His Temple Now Behold Him
Love Divine, All Loves Excelling
Of The Father's Love Begotten
Joy To The World
Thee We Adore, Eternal Lord
O Zion, Haste
Praise To The Lord, The Almighty

CYCLE C

Herald, Sound The Note Of Judgment
The Only Son From Heaven
Hark, The Glad Sound
Rejoice, O Pilgrim Throng!

Weekly Record

Date					
Entrance Hymn					
Hymn Of The Day					
Anthem/ Special Music					
Sermon Title					
Lay Reader					
Attendance					

Fourth Sunday In Advent

Readings

LESSON		CYCLE A	CYCLE B	CYCLE C
		Revised Common	**Revised Common**	**Revised Common**
First		Isaiah 7:10-16	2 Samuel 7:1-11, 16	Micah 5:2-5a
Second		Romans 1:1-7	Romans 16:25-27	Hebrews 10:5-10
Gospel		Matthew 1:18-25	Luke 1:26-38	Luke 1:39-45 (46-55)
		Episcopal	**Episcopal**	**Episcopal**
First		Isaiah 7:10-17	2 Samuel 7:4, 8-16	Micah 2:4
Second		Romans 1:1-7	Romans 16:25-27	Hebrews 10:5-10
Gospel		Matthew 1:18-25	Luke 1:26-38	Luke 1:39-49 (50-56)
		Lutheran	**Lutheran**	**Lutheran**
First		Isaiah 7:10-14 (15-17)	2 Samuel 7:(1-7) 8-11, 16	Micah 5:2-4
Second		Romans 1:1-7	Romans 16:25-27	Hebrews 10:5-10
Gospel		Matthew 1:18-25	Luke 1:26-38	Luke 1:39-45 (46-55)
		Roman Catholic	**Roman Catholic**	**Roman Catholic**
First		Isaiah 7:10-14	2 Samuel 7:1-5, 8-11, 16	Micah 5:2-5a
Second		Romans 1:1-7	Romans 16:25-27	Hebrews 10:5-10
Gospel		Matthew 1:18-24	Luke 1:26-38	Luke 1:39-45

Notes

Creed: Nicene
Color: Blue or purple
Special Notation: Prayers said by women and including women's concerns.

Special Notes For A

The prophetic message is that "a virgin shall bear a son and his name shall be called Emmanuel." Joseph is told to take Mary as his wife even though she is pregnant with a child which he did not father. Again, reference is made to the connection between the royal house of David and the Messiah.

Special Notes For B

First lesson affirms Jesus' Jewishness. Gospel could be by two people as angels and one as Mary with or without narrator. Banner: Mary (pregnant) with dove overhead. Also show Jewish symbols of Menorah, Star of David and Stem of Jesse.

Special Notes For C

Mary became the blessed one by believing the promise made her by the Lord. Those who believe the Christ child is Lord and Savior are blessed ones, too.

Music For Worship For Fourth Sunday Of Advent

NOTES	CYCLE A	CYCLE B	CYCLE C
	First Lesson Savior Of The Nations, Come What Child Is This? Of The Father's Love Begotten **Second Lesson** Come, O Precious Ransom The Bells Of Christmas Hail To The Lord's Anointed **Gospel** Savior Of The Nations, Come	(Stanzas 1, 12-14) From Heaven Above (Stanzas 1, 4-6) The Bells Of Christmas (Stanzas 1-2, 4-5) Lo, How A Rose Is Growing Come, Thou Long-Expected Jesus From East To West All Praise To You Eternal Lord Joy To The World My Soul Now Magnifies The Lord What Wondrous Love Is This My God, How Wonderful Thou Art Of The Father's Love Begotten The Only Son From Heaven	My Soul Now Magnifies The Lord Savior Of The Nations, Come Come, Thou Long-Expected Jesus **Gospel** O Little Town Of Bethlehem Savior, Like A Shepherd Lead Us

Weekly Record

Date								
Entrance Hymn								
Hymn Of The Day								
Anthem/ Special Music								
Sermon Title								
Lay Reader								
Attendance								

Christmas Eve Candlelight Service

Readings

LESSON	CYCLE A	CYCLE B	CYCLE C
	Revised Common	**Revised Common**	**Revised Common**
First	Isaiah 9:2-7	Isaiah 9:2-7	Isaiah 9:2-7
Second	Titus 2:11-14	Titus 2:11-14	Titus 2:11-14
Gospel	Luke 2:1-20	Luke 2:1-20	Luke 2:1-20
	Episcopal	**Episcopal**	**Episcopal**
First	Isaiah 9:2-4, 6-7	Isaiah 9:2-4, 6-7	Isaiah 9:2-4, 6-7
Second	Titus 2:11-14	Titus 2:11-14	Titus 2:11-14
Gospel	Luke 2:1-14 (15-20)	Luke 2:1-14 (15-20)	Luke 2:1-14 (15-20)
	Lutheran	**Lutheran**	**Lutheran**
First	Isaiah 9:2-7	Isaiah 9:2-7	Isaiah 9:2-7
Second	Titus 2:11-14	Titus 2:11-14	Titus 2:11-14
Gospel	Luke 2:1-20	Luke 2:1-20	Luke 2:1-20
	Roman Catholic	**Roman Catholic**	**Roman Catholic**
First	Isaiah 9:2-7	Isaiah 9:2-7	Isaiah 9:2-7
Second	Titus 2:11-14	Titus 2:11-14	Titus 2:11-14
Gospel	Luke 2:1-14	Luke 2:1-14	Luke 2:1-14

Notes

Creed: Nicene

Color: White

Special Notation: Prayers could reflect fascination with all the wonders of God.

Special Notes For A

A single, lighted candle may be brought in procession into the darkened church. During hymn "Joyous Light Of Glory," altar candles, tapers at pews and Christmas tree lights could be kindled. Pew candles may be lit from the great single candle and extinguished at end of hymn. Or light pew candles at end of service as sanctuary lights are dimmed and congregation sings final hymn ("Silent Night") before carrying the light of Christ out into the world.

Special Notes For B

Ceremony of Carols: alternating portions of Luke's Christmas gospel with stanzas of hymns depicting each stage of the story.

Special Notes For C

Use the following themes to identify each section of the order of worship: 1. The Community Awaits Christ's Coming. 2. The Community Celebrates Christ's Birth. 3. The Community Responds to Christ's Presence.

Music For Worship For Christmas Eve Candlelight Service

NOTES	CYCLE A	CYCLE B	CYCLE C
	He Whom Shepherds Once Come Praising Joy To The World	God, Whose Almighty Word Silent Night, Holy Night Lo, How A Rose Is Growing Hark! The Herald Angels Sing The Bells Of Christmas	From Shepherding Of Stars The Hills Are Bare At Bethlehem Away In A Manger I Am So Glad Each Christmas Eve

Weekly Record

Date						
Entrance Hymn						
Hymn Of The Day						
Anthem/ Special Music						
Sermon Title						
Lay Reader						
Attendance						

Christmas Day

Readings

LESSON	CYCLE A	CYCLE B	CYCLE C
	Revised Common	**Revised Common**	**Revised Common**
First	Isaiah 52:7-10	Isaiah 52:7-10	Isaiah 52:7-10
Second	Hebrews 1:1-4 (5-12)	Hebrews 1:1-4 (5-12)	Hebrews 1:1-4 (5-12)
Gospel	John 1:1-14	John 1:1-14	John 1:1-14
	Episcopal	**Episcopal**	**Episcopal**
First	Isaiah 52:7-10	Isaiah 52:7-10	Isaiah 52:7-10
Second	Hebrews 1:1-12	Hebrews 1:1-12	Hebrews 1:1-12
Gospel	John 1:1-14	John 1:1-14	John 1:1-14
	Lutheran	**Lutheran**	**Lutheran**
First	Isaiah 9:2-7	Isaiah 52:7-10	Isaiah 62:10-12
Second	Titus 2:11-14	Hebrews 1:1-9	Titus 3:4-7
Gospel	Luke 2:1-20	John 1:1-14	Luke 2:1-20
	Roman Catholic	**Roman Catholic**	**Roman Catholic**
First	Isaiah 52:7-10	Isaiah 52:7-10	Isaiah 52:7-10
Second	Hebrews 1:1-6	Hebrews 1:1-6	Hebrews 1:1-6
Gospel	John 1:1-18	John 1:1-18	John 1:1-18

Notes	Special Notes For A	Special Notes For B	Special Notes For C
Creed: Nicene **Color:** White **Special Notation:** Use prayers by and for children as a symbol of Christ's birth.	Talk about the mystery of Jesus' birth and the message that mystery has for us today.	Use whole loaf of bread for communion (Bethlehem means "house of bread"). Silver vessels for communion at Christmas. Decorate with poinsettias and tree with Christmons. Sunday school pageant separate from regular service.	The reading of the 1st and 2nd lessons could be done as a Herbergsuchen (German for "searching for an inn") drama. Joseph or Mary, entering at the far Narthex door and walking to left front while dressed in biblical clothing, indicating their futile attempt to find lodging. During psalm they could move to right front and the other could read second lesson. They could repeat the futility and leave by side door.

Music For Worship For Christmas Day

NOTES

CYCLE A

First Lesson
What Child Is This
O Little Town Of Bethlehem

Second Lesson
Let All Together Praise God
A Stable Lamp Is Lighted
The Only Son From Heaven

Gospel
Infant Holy, Infant Lowly
Angels, From The Realms Of Glory
It Came Upon The Midnight Clear
Silent Night, Holy Night
Angels We Have Heard On High

CYCLE B

All Praise To You, Eternal Lord
Once Again My Heart Rejoices
From Heaven Above
From Shepherding Of Stars
From East To West
Come Rejoicing, Praises Voicing
He Whom Shepherds Once Came Praising

CYCLE C

Son Of God, Eternal Savior
Once Again My Heart Rejoices
O Savior Of Our Fallen Race
Let Our Gladness Have No End
Oh, Come, All Ye Faithful
When Christmas Morn Is Dawning
All Hail To You, O Blessed Morn!

Weekly Record

Date					
Entrance Hymn					
Hymn Of The Day					
Anthem/ Special Music					
Sermon Title					
Lay Reader					
Attendance					

First Sunday After Christmas

Readings

LESSON	CYCLE A	CYCLE B	CYCLE C
	Revised Common	**Revised Common**	**Revised Common**
First	Isaiah 63:7-9	Isaiah 61:10—62:3	1 Samuel 2:18-20, 26
Second	Hebrews 2:10-18	Galatians 4:4-7	Colossians 3:12-17
Gospel	Matthew 2:13-23	Luke 2:22-40	Luke 2:41-52
	Episcopal	**Episcopal**	**Episcopal**
First	Isaiah 61:10—62:3	Isaiah 61:10—62:3	Isaiah 61:10—62:3
Second	Galatians 3:23-25; 4:4-7	Galatians 3:23-25; 4:4-7	Galatians 3:23-25; 4:4-7
Gospel	John 1:1-18	John 1:1-18	Luke 2:41-52
	Lutheran	**Lutheran**	**Lutheran**
First	Isaiah 63:7-9	Isaiah 45:22-25	Jeremiah 31:1-13
Second	Galatians 4:4-7	Colossians 3:12-17	Hebrews 2:10-18
Gospel	Matthew 2:13-15, 19-23	Luke 2:25-40	Luke 2:41-52
	Roman Catholic	**Roman Catholic**	**Roman Catholic**
First	Sirach 3:2-6, 12-14	Sirach 3:2-6, 12-14	Sirach 3:2-6, 12-14
Second	Colossians 3:12-21	Colossians 3:12-21	Colossians 3:12-21
Gospel	Matthew 2:13-15, 19-23	Luke 2:22-40	Luke 2:41-52

Notes	Special Notes For A	Special Notes For B	Special Notes For C
Creed: Nicene **Color:** White **Special Notation:** Jesus' presentation in the temple. Jesus' blessings; his parents' amazement.	Theme is angelic intervention in order to avert evil.	Special attention to Simeon's Song "Lord, Now You Let Your Servant Go In Peace" by soloist or choir. Prayers for and by senior adults on the day of Simeon and Anna or read the lesson or take gospel parts for Simeon and Anna.	A special step toward Jesus' baptism and ministry in which he draws nurture from wise teachers and leaders of the church. We should do the same.

Music For Worship For First Sunday After Christmas

NOTES	CYCLE A	CYCLE B	CYCLE C
	First Lesson Joy To The World **Second Lesson** O Savior Of Our Fallen Race I Am So Glad Each Christmas Eve Children Of The Heavenly Father **Gospel** From God The Father, Virgin Born When Christ's Appearing Was Made Known In A Lowly Manger Born	All Praise To You, Eternal Lord The Only Son From Heaven I Leave, As You Have Promised Lord Let All Mortal Flesh Keep Silence In This Temple Now Behold Him O Lord, Now Let Your Servant Our Father, By Whose Name	Sing My Tongue, The Glorious Battle Cold December Flies Away Let All Together Praise Our God All Praise To You, Eternal Lord The Only Son From Heaven

Weekly Record

Date					
Entrance Hymn					
Hymn Of The Day					
Anthem/ Special Music					
Sermon Title					
Lay Reader					
Attendance					

Second Sunday After Christmas

Readings

LESSON	CYCLE A	CYCLE B	CYCLE C
	Revised Common	**Revised Common**	**Revised Common**
First	Jeremiah 31:7-14 or Sirach 24:1-12	Jeremiah 31:7-14 or Sirach 24:1-12	Jeremiah 31:7-14 or Sirach 24:1-12
Second	Ephesians 1:3-14	Ephesians 1:3-14	Ephesians 1:3-14
Gospel	John 1:(1-9) 10-18	John 1:(1-9) 10-18	John 1:(1-9) 10-18
	Episcopal	**Episcopal**	**Episcopal**
First	Jeremiah 31:7-14	Jeremiah 31:7-14	Jeremiah 31:7-14
Second	Ephesians 1:3-6, 15-19a	Ephesians 1:3-6, 15-19a	Ephesians 1:3-6, 15-19a
Gospel	Luke 2:41-51 or Matthew 2:1-12	Luke 2:41-51 or Matthew 2:1-12	Luke 2:41-51 or Matthew 2:1-12
	Lutheran	**Lutheran**	**Lutheran**
First	Isaiah 61:10—62:3	Isaiah 61:10—62:3	Isaiah 61:10—62:3
Second	Ephesians 1:3-6, 15-18	Ephesians 1:3-6, 15-18	Ephesians 1:3-6, 15-18
Gospel	John 1:1-18	John 1:1-18	John 1:1-18
	Roman Catholic	**Roman Catholic**	**Roman Catholic**
First	Sirach 24:1-4, 8-12	Sirach 24:1-2, 8-12	Sirach 24:1-4, 8-12
Second	Ephesians 1:3-6, 15-18	Ephesians 1:3-6, 15-18	Ephesians 1:3-6, 15-18
Gospel	John 1:1-18	John 1:1-18	John 1:1-18

Notes

	Special Notes For A	Special Notes For B	Special Notes For C
	A joyful statement using wedding, coronation and agricultural images to celebrate God's action on behalf of his people, as by giving Jesus to the world he destined us in love to be his family.	We are to go forth as with the brightness of lamps. We are his adopted children and his grace has made us accepted.	These days are a time of purity and joy in remembrance of the incarnation. A time of fulfillment as the waiting is over. We give praise and affirmation of his presence among us.

Creed: Nicene
Color: White
Special Notation:

Music For Worship For Second Sunday After Christmas

NOTES

CYCLE A	CYCLE B	CYCLE C
First Lesson Joy To The World	Let All Together Praise Our God I Heard The Voice Of Jesus Say What Child Is This Angel, From The Realms Of Glory The First Noel	Of The Father's Love Begotten Let All Mortal Flesh Keep Silence He Whom Shepherds Once Came Praising Go Tell It On The Mountain
Second Lesson O Savior Of Our Fallen Race I Am So Glad Each Christmas Eve Children Of The Heavenly Father		
Gospel Of The Father's Love Begotten Oh, Come All Ye Faithful Let Our Gladness Have No End		

Weekly Record

Date						
Entrance Hymn						
Hymn Of The Day						
Anthem/ Special Music						
Sermon Title						
Lay Reader						
Attendance						

New Year's Eve / Seventh Day In The Octave Of Christmas (RC)

Readings

LESSON		CYCLE A	CYCLE B	CYCLE C
		Revised Common	**Revised Common**	**Revised Common**
First		Ecclesiastes 3:1-13	Ecclesiastes 3:1-13	Ecclesiastes 3:1-13
Second		Revelation 21:1-6a	Revelation 21:1-6a	Revelation 21:1-6a
Gospel		Matthew 25:31-46	Matthew 25:31-46	Matthew 25:31-46
		Episcopal	**Episcopal**	**Episcopal**
First		Exodus 34:1-8	Exodus 34:1-8	Exodus 34:1-8
Second		Romans 1:1-7	Romans 1:1-7	Romans 1:1-7
Gospel		Luke 2:15-21	Luke 2:15-21	Luke 2:15-21
		Lutheran	**Lutheran**	**Lutheran**
First		Jeremiah 24:1-7	Jeremiah 24:1-7	Jeremiah 24:1-7
Second		1 Peter 1:22-25	1 Peter 1:22-25	1 Peter 1:22-25
Gospel		Luke 13:6-9	Luke 13:6-9	Luke 13:6-9
		Roman Catholic	**Roman Catholic**	**Roman Catholic**
First		John 2:18-21	John 2:18-21	John 2:18-21
Gospel		John 1:1-18	John 1:1-18	John 1:1-18

Notes	Special Notes For A	Special Notes For B	Special Notes For C
	This is the 7th day of Christmas. Service of the word or vespers. Turning from past to future. Goals to set. Prayers for guidance.	Vision of the figs. Souls purified by truth and hearts purified by love. We come and go, but the Word is forever.	Parable of the fig tree. Luke is said to give us the teaching of Paul, who was his companion and from whom he derives his spirit. He accepts Jesus as Savior of all people and the satisfier of all needs.

Creed: Nicene
Color: White
Special Notation:

NOTES

CYCLE A

Greet Now The Swiftly Changing Year
O God, Our Help In Ages Past
All Depends On Our Possessing
Evening And Morning
From God Can Nothing Move Me
Come, Gracious Spirit, Heavenly Dove

CYCLE B

Greet Now The Swiftly Changing Year
O God, Our Help In Ages Past
O God Of Jacob
Oh, That The Lord Would Guide My Ways
Lord, As A Pilgrim
I Heard The Voice Of Jesus Say

CYCLE C

Greet Now The Swiftly Changing Year
O God, Our Help In Ages Past
Now Thank We All Our God
Let All Things Now Living

Weekly Record

Date			
Entrance Hymn			
Hymn Of The Day			
Anthem/ Special Music			
Sermon Title			
Lay Reader			
Attendance			

New Year's Day / Holy Name Of Jesus / Solemnity Of Mary, Mother Of God

Readings

LESSON		CYCLE A	CYCLE B	CYCLE C
		Revised Common	**Revised Common**	**Revised Common**
First		Ecclesiastes 3:1-13	Ecclesiastes 3:1-13	Ecclesiastes 3:1-13
Second		Revelation 21:1-6a	Revelation 21:1-6a	Revelation 21:1-6a
Gospel		Matthew 25:31-46	Matthew 25:31-46	Matthew 25:31-46
		Episcopal	**Episcopal**	**Episcopal**
First		Exodus 34:1-8	Exodus 34:1-8	Exodus 34:1-8
Second		Romans 1:1-7	Romans 1:1-7	Romans 1:1-7
Gospel		Luke 2:15-21	Luke 2:15-21	Luke 2:15-21
		Lutheran	**Lutheran**	**Lutheran**
First		Numbers 6:22-27	Numbers 6:22-27	Numbers 6:22-27
Second		Romans 1:1-7	Romans 1:1-7	Romans 1:1-7
Gospel		Luke 2:21	Luke 2:21	Luke 2:21
		Roman Catholic	**Roman Catholic**	**Roman Catholic**
First		Numbers 6:22-27	Numbers 6:22-27	Numbers 6:22-27
Second		Galatians 4:4-7	Galatians 4:4-7	Galatians 4:4-7
Gospel		Luke 2:16-21	Luke 2:16-21	Luke 2:16-21

Notes	Special Notes For A	Special Notes For B	Special Notes For C
Color: White **Special Notation:** Celebrate the goodness of God as you enter a new year. Pause to reflect on the blessings and growth of the past.	We stand at the crossroads between past and future. Seek forgiveness of the past: broken promises, misguided actions, deeds not done.	Focus on God's love and mercy. Look to the cross of Christ. Look in repentance to receive forgiveness.	Seek a clear vision of God's will so all may continue to celebrate salvation today and everyday.

Music For Worship For New Year's Day / Holy Name Of Jesus / Solemnity Of Mary / Mother Of God

NOTES	CYCLE A	CYCLE B	CYCLE C
	All Hail The Power Of Jesus' Name How Sweet The Name Of Jesus Sounds At The Name Of Jesus Oh, For A Thousand Tongues To Sing Oh Savior, Precious Savior	All Hail The Power Of Jesus' Name At The Name Of Jesus How Sweet The Name Of Jesus Sounds Oh For A Thousand Tongues To Sing O Savior, Precious Savior	Greet Now The Swiftly Changing Year O God, Our Help In Ages Past All Hail The Power Of Jesus' Name At The Name Of Jesus How Sweet The Name Of Jesus Sounds O Savior, Precious Savior Oh, For A Thousand Tongues To Sing

Weekly Record

Date			
Entrance Hymn			
Hymn Of The Day			
Anthem/ Special Music			
Sermon Title			
Lay Reader			
Attendance			

Epiphany Of Our Lord

Readings

LESSON	CYCLE A	CYCLE B	CYCLE C
	Revised Common	**Revised Common**	**Revised Common**
First	Isaiah 60:1-6	Isaiah 60:1-6	Isaiah 60:1-6
Second	Ephesians 3:1-12	Ephesians 3:1-12	Ephesians 3:1-12
Gospel	Matthew 2:1-12	Matthew 2:1-12	Matthew 2:1-12
	Episcopal	**Episcopal**	**Episcopal**
First	Isaiah 60:1-6, 9	Isaiah 60:1-6, 9	Isaiah 60:1-6
Second	Ephesians 3:1-12	Ephesians 3:1-12	Ephesians 3:1-12
Gospel	Matthew 2:1-12	Matthew 2:1-12	Matthew 2:1-12
	Lutheran	**Lutheran**	**Lutheran**
First	Isaiah 60:1-6	Isaiah 60:1-6	Isaiah 60:1-6
Second	Ephesians 3:2-12	Ephesians 3:2-12	Ephesians 3:2-12
Gospel	Matthew 2:1-12	Matthew 2:1-12	Matthew 2:1-12
	Roman Catholic	**Roman Catholic**	**Roman Catholic**
First	Isaiah 60:1-6	Isaiah 60:1-6	Isaiah 60:1-6
Second	Ephesians 3:2-3a, 5-6	Ephesians 3:2-3a, 5-6	Ephesians 3:2-3, 5-6
Gospel	Matthew 2:1-12	Matthew 2:1-12	Matthew 2:1-12

Special Notes For A

Epiphany of Our Lord was first celebrated in the 4th century for the birth of Christ and in the 6th century became focused on his baptism.

Special Notes For B

Epiphany has a three-fold emphasis — the star leading the magi, the baptism of Jesus in the Jordan and his changing of water to wine at Cana. First revelation to the gentiles (magi) leads to emphasis on missionary work. We should think of the many times and many ways God has been with us.

Special Notes For C

The community prays this day for the full vision of life produced by the revelation of Christ. The gospel discusses Christ as Lord of the universe. The church is on a pilgrimage. The chasuble is a symbol that the church is clothed for its journey. A processional cross could be used to show the people of God set in motion. Torches capture the theme of the light of God as a lamp directing our way.

Notes

Creed: Nicene
Color: White or gold
Special Notation: A fitting time for baptism. The image is light. The Star of Bethlehem and Christ candle are valid symbols.

Music For Worship For The Epiphany Of Our Lord

NOTES

CYCLE A	CYCLE B	CYCLE C
Brightest And Best Of The Stars Of The Morning Bright And Glorious Is The Sky As With Gladness Men Of Old O God Of Life's Great Mystery	Bright And Glorious Is The Sky Brightest And Best Of The Stars Of The Morning God, Whose Almighty Word When Christ's Appearing Was Made Known To Jordan Came The Christ, Our Lord Angels, From The Realms Of Glory Christ, Whose Glory Fills The Skies O Christ, You Are The Light And Day O God Of God, O Light Of Light Oh, For A Thousand Tongues To Sing In A Lowly Manger Born Rise, Shine, You People!	Bright And Glorious Is The Sky Brightest And Best Of The Stars Of The Morning Angels From The Realms Of Glory Christ, Whose Glory Fills The Skies O Splendor Of The Father's Light O Christ, You Are The Light And Day Oh, For A Thousand Tongues To Sing

Weekly Record

Date				
Entrance Hymn				
Hymn Of The Day				
Anthem/Special Music				
Sermon Title				
Lay Reader				
Attendance				

First Sunday After Epiphany

Readings

LESSON		CYCLE A	CYCLE B	CYCLE C
		Revised Common	**Revised Common**	**Revised Common**
First		Isaiah 42:1-9	Genesis 1:1-5	Isaiah 43:1-7
Second		Acts 10:34-43	Acts 19:1-7	Acts 8:14-17
Gospel		Matthew 3:13-17	Mark 1:4-11	Luke 3:15-17, 21-22
		Episcopal	**Episcopal**	**Episcopal**
First		Isaiah 42:1-9	Isaiah 42:1-9	Isaiah 42:1-9
Second		Acts 10:34-48	Acts 10:34-48	Acts 10:34-38
Gospel		Matthew 3:13-17	Mark 1:7-11	Luke 3:15-16, 21-22
		Lutheran	**Lutheran**	**Lutheran**
First		Isaiah 42:1-7	Isaiah 42:1-7	Isaiah 42:1-7
Second		Acts 10:34-38	Acts 10:34-38	Acts 10:34-38
Gospel		Matthew 3:13-17	Mark 1:4-11	Luke 3:15-17, 21-22
		Roman Catholic	**Roman Catholic**	**Roman Catholic**
First		Isaiah 42:1-4, 6-7	Isaiah 42:1-4, 6-7	Isaiah 42:1-4, 6-7
Second		Acts 10:34-38	Acts 10:34-38	Acts 10:34-38
Gospel		Matthew 3:13-17	Mark 1:7-11	Luke 3:15-16, 21-22

Notes

Creed: Nicene

Color: White

Special Notation: If no one is being baptized, the baptismal nature of the day might still be expressed.

Special Notes For A

John was reluctant to baptize Jesus, feeling unworthy and wishing Jesus were baptizing him. Many people chosen to work for the Lord felt the same way, but God requires obedience even when understanding is absent. The gospel words can hardly hold their enormous meaning. Sacrament of Baptism is appropriate for today.

Special Notes For B

Accent on "seeing" the gospel. God became one of us to help us see. Posters, bulletins or banners can portray God's becoming human. Slides or paintings or prints may be shown.

Special Notes For C

We are joined to the community of Christ, sealed in his kingdom. It shows God's promises fulfilled, the power of the Spirit in the church and Jesus as king of creation. Pray for world missionaries at the same time we pray for those who patrol the streets, teach the children and govern the courts. Do not forget council members, Sunday school teachers and members of clergy.

Music For Worship For First Sunday After Epiphany

NOTES	CYCLE A	CYCLE B	CYCLE C
	Hail To The Lord's Anointed We Know That Christ Is Raised From God The Father, Virgin-Born God, Whose Almighty Word When Christ's Appearing Was Made Known	From God The Father, Virgin-Born The Only Son From Heaven I Bind Unto Myself Today Bright And Glorious Is The Sky O Chief Of Cities, Bethlehem As With Gladness Men Of Old Brightest And Best Of The Stars Of The Morning	On Jordan's Banks The Baptist's Cry From God The Father, Virgin-Born When Christ's Appearing Was Made Known All Who Believe And Are Baptized This Is The Spirit's Entry Now Eternal Ruler Of The Ceaseless Round

Weekly Record

Date				
Entrance Hymn				
Hymn Of The Day				
Anthem/ Special Music				
Sermon Title				
Lay Reader				
Attendance				

Second Sunday After Epiphany

Readings

LESSON	CYCLE A	CYCLE B	CYCLE C
	Revised Common	**Revised Common**	**Revised Common**
First	Isaiah 49:1-7	1 Samuel 3:1-10 (11-20)	Isaiah 62:1-5
Second	1 Corinthians 1:1-9	1 Corinthians 6:12-20	1 Corinthians 12:1-11
Gospel	John 1:29-42	John 1:43-51	John 2:1-11
	Episcopal	**Episcopal**	**Episcopal**
First	Isaiah 49:1-7	1 Samuel 3:1-10 (11-20)	Isaiah 62:1-5
Second	1 Corinthians 1:1-9	1 Corinthians 6:11b-20	1 Corinthians 12:1-11
Gospel	John 1:29-41	John 1:43-51	John 2:1-11
	Lutheran	**Lutheran**	**Lutheran**
First	Isaiah 49:1-6	1 Samuel 3:1-10	Isaiah 62:1-5
Second	1 Corinthians 1:1-9	1 Corinthians 6:12-20	1 Corinthians 12:1-11
Gospel	John 1:29-41	John 1:43-51	John 2:1-11
	Roman Catholic	**Roman Catholic**	**Roman Catholic**
First	Isaiah 49:3, 5-6	1 Samuel 3:3-10, 19	Isaiah 62:1-5
Second	1 Corinthians 1:1-13	1 Corinthians 6:13-15, 17-20	1 Corinthians 12:4-11
Gospel	John 1:29-34	John 1:35-42	John 2:1-12

Notes

Creed: Apostles'
Color: Green
Special Notation: Color is living, growing plant suggesting spiritual growth. Theme is the healing and restorative power of God's love.

Special Notes For A

This is like instant replay from the other side of the field. This time we look through eyes of faith recognizing Jesus as the Son of God. How can we give our members a chance to make a statement of faith? Can some be drawn closer?

Special Notes For B

Are we sharing the good news with others? How can we help practicing Christians mobilize resources for witnessing to the non-practicing members of their families?

Special Notes For C

Discuss visitation of sick, counseling and reuniting of sinners made whole in community of Christ. The themes show Christ, a person of compassion and mercy; his revelation in human events; God's reunion with his people and the restoration of his kingdom.

Music For Worship For Second Sunday After Epiphany

NOTES	CYCLE A	CYCLE B	CYCLE C
	Lord, Speak To Us, That We May Speak I Love To Tell The Story Lift Every Voice And Sing Sent Forth By God's Blessing The Only Son From Heaven All Praise To You, O Lord Jesus, Priceless Treasure	Jesus Calls Us, O'er The Tumult May God Bestow On Us This Grace By All Your Saints In Warfare	The Only Son From Heaven Jesus, Priceless Treasure Jesus Calls Us, O'er the Tumult

Weekly Record

Date						
Entrance Hymn						
Hymn Of The Day						
Anthem/ Special Music						
Sermon Title						
Lay Reader						
Attendance						

Third Sunday After Epiphany

Readings

LESSON		CYCLE A	CYCLE B	CYCLE C
		Revised Common	**Revised Common**	**Revised Common**
First		Isaiah 9:1-4	Jonah 3:1-5, 10	Nehemiah 8:1-3, 5-6, 8-10
Second		1 Corinthians 1:10-18	1 Corinthians 7:29-31	1 Corinthians 12:12-31a
Gospel		Matthew 4:12-23	Mark 1:14-20	Luke 4:14-21
		Episcopal	**Episcopal**	**Episcopal**
First		Amos 3:1-8	Jeremiah 3:21—4:2	Nehemiah 8:2-10
Second		1 Corinthians 1:10-17	1 Corinthians 7:17-23	1 Corinthians 12:12-27
Gospel		Matthew 4:12-23	Mark 1:14-20	Luke 4:14-21
		Lutheran	**Lutheran**	**Lutheran**
First		Isaiah 9:1b-4	Jonah 3:1-5, 10	Isaiah 61:1-6
Second		1 Corinthians 1:10-17	1 Corinthians 7:29-31	1 Corinthians 12:12-21, 26-27
Gospel		Matthew 4:12-23	Mark 1:14-20	Luke 4:14-21
		Roman Catholic	**Roman Catholic**	**Roman Catholic**
First		Isaiah 8:23—9:3	Jonah 3:1-5, 10	Nehemiah 8:1-4, 5-6, 8-10
Second		1 Corinthians 1:10-13, 17	1 Corinthians 7:29-31	1 Corinthians 12:12-30
Gospel		Matthew 4:12-23	Mark 1:14-20	Luke 1:1-4; 4:14-21

Notes	Special Notes For A	Special Notes For B	Special Notes For C
Creed: Apostles' **Color:** Green **Special Notation:**	This is a mission text with marching orders. Darkness has given way to light and our ordinary occupations can be transformed in the Lord's service. (A good day for a congregational meeting.)	This is a time of calling people to service in the Lord, just as Jesus did. When asked, "by what authority do you call others to serve?" be sure it is made known that not only is Jesus your authority, but that he has charged all of us to do so.	Teaching ministry is central but we need to ask: How do we bring good news to the afflicted? How do we bind up the broken-hearted? How do we proclaim liberty to the captives? Parish meetings discuss mission to the world and to their specific parish. What does it mean to be part of the kingdom of God?

Music For Worship For Third Sunday After Epiphany

NOTES	CYCLE A	CYCLE B	CYCLE C
	They Cast Their Nets The Church Of Christ, In Every Age Come, Let Us Eat Rise Up, O Saints Of God! O God Of Light Hail To The Lord's Anointed O Christ, Our Light, O Radiance True	O God Of Light "Come Follow Me," The Savior Spake By All Your Saints In Warfare Jesus Calls Us, O'er The Tumult God, Whose Almighty Word From God The Father, Virgin Born O One With God The Father O Morning Star, How Fair And Bright!	O God Of Light O Christ, Our Light, O Radiance True "Come Follow Me," The Savior Spake O Trinity, O Blessed Light Through The Night Of Doubt And Sorrow The Church's One Foundation O Christ, The Healer, We Have Come Once He Came In Blessing

Weekly Record

Date						
Entrance Hymn						
Hymn Of The Day						
Anthem/ Special Music						
Sermon Title						
Lay Reader						
Attendance						

Fourth Sunday After Epiphany

Readings

LESSON	CYCLE A	CYCLE B	CYCLE C
	Revised Common	**Revised Common**	**Revised Common**
First	Micah 6:1-8	Deuteronomy 18:15-20	Jeremiah 1:4-10
Second	1 Corinthians 1:18-31	1 Corinthians 8:1-13	1 Corinthians 13:1-13
Gospel	Matthew 5:1-12	Mark 1:21-28	Luke 4:21-30
	Episcopal	**Episcopal**	**Episcopal**
First	Micah 6:1-8	Deuteronomy 18:15-20	Jeremiah 1:4-10
Second	1 Corinthians 1:(18-25) 26-31	1 Corinthians 8:1b-13	1 Corinthians 14:12b-20
Gospel	Matthew 5:1-12	Mark 1:21-28	Luke 4:21-32
	Lutheran	**Lutheran**	**Lutheran**
First	Micah 6:1-8	Deuteronomy 18:15-20	Jeremiah 1:4-10
Second	1 Corinthians 1:26-31	1 Corinthians 8:1-13	1 Corinthians 12:27—13:13
Gospel	Matthew 5:1-12	Mark 1:21-28	Luke 4:21-32
	Roman Catholic	**Roman Catholic**	**Roman Catholic**
First	Zephaniah 2:3, 3:12-13	Deuteronomy 18:15-20	Jeremiah 1:4-5, 17-19
Second	1 Corinthians 1:26-31	1 Corinthians 7:32-35	1 Corinthians 12:31—13:13
Gospel	Matthew 5:1-12a	Mark 1:21-28	Luke 4:21-30

Notes	Special Notes For A	Special Notes For B	Special Notes For C
Cred: Nicene **Color:** Green **Special Notation:** Invite a teacher to give the message; have him tell the children what it's like to be a teacher.	It's a blessing to know you can't make it alone. The Beatitudes should be taken literally. Our hearts should not only accept, but also imitate the way God wants the world to be ordered.	Use corporate confession and forgiveness today and urge use of individual confession and forgiveness throughout the week. Its use is a renewing of our baptism wherein the death to life process is shown and God identifies his own.	Theme focuses on our dependence on Christ. Too often we separate ourselves from the source of light and strength. Without God's help we can do nothing.

Music For Worship For Fourth Sunday After Epiphany

NOTES	CYCLE A	CYCLE B	CYCLE C
	Lord Of Glory, You Have Bought Us Where Charity And Love Prevail Let Us Break Bread Together He Leadeth Me: Oh, Blessed Thought! Hope Of The World Dear Christians, One And All God Of Grace And God Of Glory Songs Of Thankfulness And Praise	Dear Christians, One And All Songs Of Thankfulness And Praise Your Word, O Lord, Is Gentle Dew O God, My Faithful God O Christ, The Healer, We Have Come God Of Our Life, All-Glorious Lord The Only Son From Heaven	Songs Of Thankfulness And Praise Dear Christians, One And All Song Of God, Eternal Savior Hope Of The World

Weekly Record

Date					
Entrance Hymn					
Hymn Of The Day					
Anthem/ Special Music					
Sermon Title					
Lay Reader					
Attendance					

Fifth Sunday After Epiphany

Readings

LESSON	CYCLE A	CYCLE B	CYCLE C
	Revised Common	**Revised Common**	**Revised Common**
First	Isaiah 58:1-9a (9b-12)	Isaiah 40:21-31	Isaiah 6:1-8 (9-13)
Second	1 Corinthians 2:1-12 (13-16)	1 Corinthians 9:16-23	1 Corinthians 15:1-11
Gospel	Matthew 5:13-20	Mark 1:29-39	Luke 5:1-11
	Episcopal	**Episcopal**	**Episcopal**
First	Habakkuk 3:1-6, 17-19	2 Kings 4:(8-17) 18-21 (22-31) 32-37	Judges 6:11-24a
Second	1 Corinthians 2:1-11	1 Corinthians 9:16-23	1 Corinthians 15:1-11
Gospel	Matthew 5:13-20	Mark 1:29-39	Luke 5:1-11
	Lutheran	**Lutheran**	**Lutheran**
First	Isaiah 58:5-9a	Job 7:1-7	Isaiah 6:1-8 (9-13)
Second	1 Corinthians 2:1-5	1 Corinthians 9:16-23	1 Corinthians 14:12b-20
Gospel	Matthew 5:13-20	Mark 1:29-39	Luke 5:1-11
	Roman Catholic	**Roman Catholic**	**Roman Catholic**
First	Isaiah 58:7-10	Job 7:1-4, 6-7	Isaiah 6:1-8
Second	1 Corinthians 2:1-5	1 Corinthians 9:15-19, 22-23	1 Corinthians 15:1-11
Gospel	Matthew 5:13-16	Mark 1:29-39	Luke 5:1-11

Notes	Special Notes For A	Special Notes For B	Special Notes For C
Cred: Apostles' **Color:** Green **Special Notation:** Presentation of various ministries of members.	Does our church affect life in our community? Would people miss us if we weren't there? Does anyone need what we have to offer?	Job spoke in anguish and wished for death. Do we not see the same today in the homeless, the hungry, the sick and elderly? A missions committee might be appointed to prepare a list of names and addresses and ways of helping the poor and afflicted locally, nationwide and worldwide, asking members to adopt at least one for year-round sharing.	Offertory could be stressed. We offer ourselves and time as well as our treasures in response to gospel. Opportunities to serve the needs of the saints are better incorporated into liturgy than as public announcements.

Music For Worship For Fifth Sunday After Epiphany

NOTES	CYCLE A	CYCLE B	CYCLE C
	God Of Grace And God Of Glory Lord, Speak To Us, That We May Speak Praise God, Praise Him On Our Way Rejoicing Hail To The Lord's Anointed O Christ The Healer, We Have Come Your Word, O Lord, Is Gentle Dew	O Christ, The Healer, We Have Come Your Word, O Lord, Is Gentle Dew Jesus, Still Lead On God, My Lord, My Strength What Wonderous Love Is This I Love To Tell The Story O Zion Haste Look From Your Sphere Of Endless Day Rise, Shine, You People! God! Whose Almighty Word Your Hand, O Lord In Days Of Old My Soul! Now Praise Your Maker!	Hail To The Lord's Anointed Your Word, O Lord, Is Gentle Dew May We Your Precepts, Lord, Fulfill O Christ, The Healer, We Have Come

Weekly Record

Date							
Entrance Hymn							
Hymn Of The Day							
Anthem/ Special Music							
Sermon Title							
Lay Reader							
Attendance							

Sixth Sunday After Epiphany

Readings

LESSON	CYCLE A	CYCLE B	CYCLE C
	Revised Common	**Revised Common**	**Revised Common**
First	Deuteronomy 30:15-20 or Sirach 15:15-20	2 Kings 5:1-14	Jeremiah 17:5-10
Second	1 Corinthians 3:1-9	1 Corinthians 9:24-27	1 Corinthians 15:12-20
Gospel	Matthew 5:21-37	Mark 1:40-45	Luke 6:17-26
	Episcopal	**Episcopal**	**Episcopal**
First	Ecclesiasticus 15:11-20	2 Kings 5:1-15	Jeremiah 17:5-10
Second	1 Corinthians 3:1-9	1 Corinthians 9:24-27	1 Corinthians 15:12-20
Gospel	Matthew 5:21-24, 27-30, 33-37	Mark 1:40-45	Luke 6:17-26
	Lutheran	**Lutheran**	**Lutheran**
First	Deuteronomy 30:15-20	2 Kings 5:1-14	Jeremiah 17:5-8
Second	1 Corinthians 2:6-13	1 Corinthians 9:24-27	1 Corinthians 15:12, 16-20
Gospel	Matthew 5:20-37	Mark 1:40-45	Luke 6:17-26
	Roman Catholic	**Roman Catholic**	**Roman Catholic**
First	Sirach 15:15-20	Leviticus 13:1-2, 44-46	Jeremiah 17:5-8
Second	1 Corinthians 2:6-10	1 Corinthians 10:31—11:1	1 Corinthians 15:12, 16-20
Gospel	Matthew 5:17-37	Mark 1:40-45	Luke 6:17, 20-26

Notes	Special Notes For A	Special Notes For B	Special Notes For C
Creed: Apostles' **Color:** Green **Special Notation:** God has sent Christ to bring healing, liberation, salvation, to the world, the world which God loves, and asks us to do the same.	The text points to royal authority and shows us Jesus' awareness of our human capacity for self-deception.	Paul likens his self-denial in life to a person who trains for a race. He urges us to be temperate in all things. The prize he hopes to win is the ultimate one.	We are reminded that those who profess to be self-made and give credit of success to their own cleverness and things of humankind place their trust in the world. "Woe unto" and "cursed be" are the Lord's pronouncement for them.

Music For Worship For Sixth Sunday After Epiphany

NOTES	CYCLE A	CYCLE B	CYCLE C
	Dearest Jesus, At Your Word Oh, That The Lord Would Guide My Ways Here, O My Lord, I See Thee Let Us Ever Walk With Jesus O Christ, Our Hope O Jesus Christ, May Grateful Hymns Be Rising	O Jesus Christ, May Grateful Hymns Be Rising Oh, That The Lord Would Guide My Ways God The Father, Be Our Stay Fight The Good Fight Thee Will I Love, My Strength Songs Of Thankfulness And Praise O Christ, The Healer, We Have Come Your Hand, O Lord, In Days Of Old O God, Whose Will Is Life And Good	O Christ, Our Hope Lord Jesus Think On Me Oh, That The Lord Would Guide My Ways Amid The World's Bleak Wilderness I Am Trusting You, Lord Jesus Your Word, O Lord, Is Gentle Dew Christ Is Arisen Jesus Christ, My Sure Defense I Know Of A Sleep In Jesus' Name I Know That My Redeemer Lives! Arise, My Soul, Arise How Blest Are Those Who Know Their Need Of God

Weekly Record

Date					
Entrance Hymn					
Hymn Of The Day					
Anthem/ Special Music					
Sermon Title					
Lay Reader					
Attendance					

Seventh Sunday After Epiphany

Readings

LESSON	CYCLE A	CYCLE B	CYCLE C
	Revised Common	**Revised Common**	**Revised Common**
First	Leviticus 19:1-2, 9-18	2 Kings 2:1-12	Genesis 45:3-11, 15
Second	1 Corinthians 3:10-11, 16-23	2 Corinthians 4:3-6	1 Corinthians 15:35-38, 42-50
Gospel	Matthew 5:38-48	Mark 9:2-9	Luke 6:27-38
	Episcopal	**Episcopal**	**Episcopal**
First	Leviticus 19:1-2, 9-18	1 Kings 19:9-18	Genesis 45:3-11, 21-28
Second	1 Corinthians 3:10-11, 16-23	2 Peter 1:16-19 (20-21)	1 Corinthians 15:35-38, 42-50
Gospel	Matthew 5:38-48	Mark 9:2-9	Luke 6:27-38
	Lutheran	**Lutheran**	**Lutheran**
First	Leviticus 19:1-2, 17-18	Isaiah 43:18-25	Genesis 45:3-8a, 15
Second	1 Corinthians 3:10-11, 16-23	2 Corinthians 1:18-22	1 Corinthians 15:35-38a, 42-50
Gospel	Matthew 5:38-48	Mark 2:1-12	Luke 6:27-38
	Roman Catholic	**Roman Catholic**	**Roman Catholic**
First	Leviticus 19:1-2, 17-18	Leviticus 19:1-2, 17-18	1 Samuel 26:2, 7-9, 12-13, 22-23
Second	1 Corinthians 3:16-23	1 Corinthians 3:16-23	1 Corinthians 15:45-59
Gospel	Matthew 5:38-48	Matthew 5:38-48	Luke 6:27-38

Notes	Special Notes For A	Special Notes For B	Special Notes For C
Creed: Apostles' **Color:** Green **Special Notation:**	The gospel theme is strength of character. Beware of the world's standards: power over others, status, economic security. These things lead nowhere. Only by the power of the Spirit can we hope to find the genuine strength to live like citizens of heaven.	Jesus treated sins as well as sickness. Sins were forgiven and the sick were made well at his Word. All that the afflicted gave was their faith.	Jesus tells us giving and forgiving should be free, also lending and loving and kindness and mercy.

Music For Worship For Seventh Sunday After Advent

NOTES

CYCLE A

O God Of Mercy, God Of Light
In Thee Is Gladness
Lord Jesus Christ, We Humbly Pray
O God, Our Help In Ages Past
Oh, Love, How Deep
Lord, Keep Us Steadfast In Your Word

CYCLE B

Oh, Love, How Deep
Lord, Keep Us Steadfast In Your Word
Songs Of Thankfulness And Praise
O Christ, The Healer, We Have Come
O God, O Lord Of Heaven And Earth

CYCLE C

Oh, Love, How Deep
Lord, Keep Us Steadfast In Your Word
Jesus Lives! The Victory's Won
Now The Green Blade Rises
In Adam We Have All Been One
Praise And Thanks And Adoration
Lord Of All Nations, Grant The Grace

Weekly Record

Date				
Entrance Hymn				
Hymn Of The Day				
Anthem/ Special Music				
Sermon Title				
Lay Reader				
Attendance				

Eighth Sunday After Epiphany

Readings

LESSON	CYCLE A	CYCLE B	CYCLE C
	Revised Common	**Revised Common**	**Revised Common**
First	Isaiah 49:8-16a	Hosea 2:14-20	Isaiah 55:10-13
Second	1 Corinthians 4:1-5	2 Corinthians 3:1-6	1 Corinthians 15:51-58
Gospel	Matthew 6:24-34	Mark 2:13-22	Luke 6:39-49
	Episcopal	**Episcopal**	**Episcopal**
First	Isaiah 49:8-18	Hosea 2:14-23	Jeremiah 7:1-7
Second	1 Corinthians 4:1-5	2 Corinthians 3:4-11	1 Corinthians 15:50-58
Gospel	Matthew 6:24-34	Mark 2:18-22	Luke 6:39-49
	Lutheran	**Lutheran**	**Lutheran**
First	Isaiah 49:13-18	Hosea 2:14-20	Jeremiah 7:1-15
Second	1 Corinthians 4:1-13	2 Corinthians 3:1b-6	1 Corinthians 15:51-58
Gospel	Matthew 6:24-34	Mark 2:18-22	Luke 6:39-49
	Roman Catholic	**Roman Catholic**	**Roman Catholic**
First	Isaiah 49:14-15	Hosea 2:16-17, 21-22	Sirach 27:4-7
Second	1 Corinthians 4:1-5	2 Corinthians 3:1-6	1 Corinthians 15:51-58
Gospel	Matthew 6:24-34	Mark 2:18-22	Luke 6:39-45

Notes	Special Notes For A	Special Notes For B	Special Notes For C
Creed: Apostles' **Color:** Green **Special Notation:** The discipline of fasting.	Worry and anxiety about tomorrow tyrannize our existence. Jesus confronts that anxiety as one who offers changeless meaning for life.	Jesus warns that things are going to necessarily be different when he's no longer with the disciples. So often we resist change. Paul reminds us that it is the spirit, not the letter, that gives us life.	Paul again tells about change in all believers. Flesh and blood will be changed either by death or on the last day. Jesus says, "Every tree is known by his own fruit." Surely then love brings good works and evil brings corruption.

Music For Worship For Eighth Sunday After Epiphany

NOTES	CYCLE A	CYCLE B	CYCLE C
	Dear Lord And Father Of Mankind If You Put Trust In God To Guide You O Living Bread From Heaven With The Lord Begin Your Task Sing Praise To God, The Highest God Salvation Unto Us Has Come O God Of Mercy, God Of Light As With Gladness Men Of Old	Salvation Unto Us Has Come As With Gladness Men Of Old When In The Hour Of Deepest Need Son Of God, Eternal Savior O God Of Love, O King Of Peace Praise To The Lord, The Almighty Praise, My Soul, The King Of Heaven	As With Gladness Men Of Old Salvation Unto Us Has Come Jesus, Priceless Treasure Sing, Praise To God, The Highest God

Weekly Record

Date					
Entrance Hymn					
Hymn Of The Day					
Anthem/ Special Music					
Sermon Title					
Lay Reader					
Attendance					

Transfiguration Of Our Lord

Readings

LESSON	CYCLE A	CYCLE B	CYCLE C
	Revised Common	**Revised Common**	**Revised Common**
First	Exodus 24:12-18	2 Kings 2:1-12	Exodus 34:29-35
Second	2 Peter 1:16-21	2 Corinthians 4:3-6	2 Corinthians 3:12—4:2
Gospel	Matthew 17:1-9	Mark 9:2-9	Luke 9:28-36
	Episcopal	**Episcopal**	**Episcopal**
First	Exodus 24:12 (13-14) 15-18	1 Kings 19:9-18	Exodus 34:29-35
Second	Philippians 3:7-14	2 Peter 1:16-19	1 Corinthians 12:27—13:13
Gospel	Matthew 17:1-9	Mark 9:2-9	Luke 9:28-36
	Lutheran	**Lutheran**	**Lutheran**
First	Exodus 24:12, 15-18	2 Kings 2:1-12a	Deuteronomy 34:1-12
Second	2 Peter 1:16-19	2 Corinthians 3:12—4:2	2 Corinthians 4:3-6
Gospel	Matthew 17:1-9	Mark 9:2-9	Luke 9:28-36
	Roman Catholic	**Roman Catholic**	**Roman Catholic**
First	Exodus 24:12, 15-18	2 Kings 2:1-12	Deuteronomy 34:1-12
Second	2 Peter 1:16-19 (20-21)	2 Corinthians 3:12—4:2	2 Corinthians 4:3-6
Gospel	Matthew 17:1-9	Mark 9:2-9	Luke 9:28-36

Notes	Special Notes For A	Special Notes For B	Special Notes For C
Creed: Nicene **Color:** White **Special Notation:** Conclusion of Epiphany and inauguration of Lent.	The disciples knew this scene on the mountain was radically different, but couldn't find a way to respond to the occasion. Words, alone, cannot capture all there is to the worship of God. Perhaps we ought to include silence, wonder, mystery, poetry, sound, aroma and color.	Believers of the Old Testament who have not turned to Jesus still have the veil of Moses upon their hearts. But we who have accepted the ministry of the Lord have renounced hidden things and have the liberty to speak plainly. The transfiguration must have been breath-taking and an awesome experience for Peter, James and John.	There is tension between the glory of God and the struggle of God, between our devotion and our mission, between the old and the new, between glory and the cross. Christ's commission is "Go in Peace. Serve the Lord." and the church's life is lived out with the orphans who need to be fed and the widows who need to be consoled.

Music For Worship For Transfiguration Of Our Lord

NOTES

CYCLE A	CYCLE B	CYCLE C
All Hail The Power Of Jesus' Name! How Good, Lord, To Be Here! O Christ, Our Hope God The Omnipotent! O God Of God, O Light Of Light	How Good, Lord, To Be Here! O God Of God, O Light Of Light Renew Me, O Eternal Light	How Good, Lord, To Be Here! O God Of God, O Light Of Light God, Whose Almighty Word

Weekly Record

Date				
Entrance Hymn				
Hymn Of The Day				
Anthem/ Special Music				
Sermon Title				
Lay Reader				
Attendance				

Ash Wednesday

Readings

LESSON	CYCLE A	CYCLE B	CYCLE C
	Revised Common	**Revised Common**	**Revised Common**
First	Joel 2:1-2, 12-17 or Isaiah 58:1-12	Joel 2:1-2, 12-17 or Isaiah 58:1-12	Joel 2:1-2, 12-17 or Isaiah 58:1-12
Second	2 Corinthians 5:20b—6:10	2 Corinthians 5:20b—6:10	2 Corinthians 5:20b—6:10
Gospel	Matthew 6:1-6, 16-21	Matthew 6:1-6, 16-21	Matthew 6:1-6, 16-21
	Episcopal	**Episcopal**	**Episcopal**
First	Joel 2:1-2, 12-17 or Isaiah 58:1-12	Joel 2:1-2, 12-17 or Isaiah 58:1-12	Joel 2:1-2, 12-17 or Isaiah 58:1-12
Second	2 Corinthians 5:20b—6:10	2 Corinthians 5:20b—6:10	2 Corinthians 5:20b—6:10
Gospel	Matthew 6:1-6, 16-21	Matthew 6:1-6, 16-21	Matthew 6:1-6, 16-21
	Lutheran	**Lutheran**	**Lutheran**
First	Joel 2:12-19	Joel 2:12-19	Joel 2:12-19
Second	2 Corinthians 5:20b—6:2	2 Corinthians 5:20b—6:2	2 Corinthians 5:20b—6:2
Gospel	Matthew 6:1-6, 16-21	Matthew 6:1-6, 16-21	Matthew 6:1-6, 16-21
	Roman Catholic	**Roman Catholic**	**Roman Catholic**
First	Joel 2:12-19	Joel 2:12-19	Joel 2:12-19
Second	2 Corinthians 5:20b—6:2	2 Corinthians 5:20b—6:2	2 Corinthians 5:20b—6:2
Gospel	Matthew 6:1-6, 16-18	Matthew 6:1-6, 16-18	Matthew 6:1-6, 16-18

Notes	Special Notes For A	Special Notes For B	Special Notes For C
Cred: Apostles' **Color:** Purple **Special Notation:** First day of Lent	The gathered community makes a personal commitment to meekness, to humility, to dependency on God's grace. The congregation draws away, apart, not caring who does or does not notice the fasting, as the Word instructs.	Ashes suggest dust, to which we shall return, also cleansing and renewal as they were once used in place of soap. It is a penitential substitute for water which both stifles and refreshes, drowns and makes alive. The custom of burning fields to ashes in Spring to destroy the old and prepare for the new tells of death and renewal.	Combines preparation for baptism and penitential reconciliation. The goal is Easter. We admit sin and we are penitent. We need the reconciliation which takes place at the foot of the cross. The theme is clear: renewal of the whole person through outer disciplines and reconciliation with God.

Music For Worship For Ash Wednesday

NOTES	CYCLE A	CYCLE B	CYCLE C
	O Lord, Throughout These Forty Days Savior, When In Dust To You Out Of The Depths I Cry To You	O Lord, Throughout These Forty Days Savior, When In Dust To You To You, Omniscient Lord Of All	Savior, When In Dust To You O Lord, Throughout These Forty Days Today Your Mercy Calls Us

Weekly Record

Date			
Entrance Hymn			
Hymn Of The Day			
Anthem/ Special Music			
Sermon Title			
Lay Reader			
Attendance			

First Sunday In Lent

Readings

LESSON		CYCLE A	CYCLE B	CYCLE C
		Revised Common	**Revised Common**	**Revised Common**
First		Genesis 2:15-17; 3:1-7	Genesis 9:8-17	Deuteronomy 26:1-11
Second		Romans 5:12-19	1 Peter 3:18-22	Romans 10:8b-13
Gospel		Matthew 4:1-11	Mark 1:9-15	Luke 4:1-13
		Episcopal	**Episcopal**	**Episcopal**
First		Genesis 2:4b-9, 15-17, 25:3:7	Genesis 9:8-17	Deuteronomy 26:(1-4) 5-11
Second		Romans 5:12-19 (20-21)	1 Peter 3:18-22	Romans 20:(5-8a) 8b-13
Gospel		Matthew 4:1-11	Mark 1:9-13	Luke 4:1-13
		Lutheran	**Lutheran**	**Lutheran**
First		Genesis 2:7-9, 15-17; 3:1-7	Genesis 22:1-18	Deuteronomy 26:5-10
Second		Romans 5:12(13-16), 17-19	Romans 8:31-39	Romans 10:8b-13
Gospel		Matthew 4:1-11	Mark 1:12-15	Luke 4:1-13
		Roman Catholic	**Roman Catholic**	**Roman Catholic**
First		Genesis 2:7-9; 3:1-7	Genesis 9:8-15	Deuteronomy 26:4-10
Second		Romans 5:12-19	1 Peter 3:18-22	Romans 10:8-13
Gospel		Matthew 4:1-11	Mark 1:12-15	Luke 4:1-13

Notes	Special Notes For A	Special Notes For B	Special Notes For C
Cred: Nicene **Color:** Purple **Special Notation:** The places of temptation are also places where God is present. If we walk in the wilderness we, too, could turn our lives around.	A Day of contrasts, between Adam and Jesus, between one who yields to temptation to be his own god and one who struggles to remain faithful. By depending on the power of the Word of God, Jesus chooses to remain close to the Father and is able to continue in his purpose to give his life and to be raised to a new life.	God's sacrifice of his only son is better understood in the account of Abraham and Isaac on Mount Moriah. A father and son, barefoot and wearing burlap could mime actions of Old Testament reading. Also, if someone is familiar with sign language, this could be another way to "hear" the gospel.	Jesus reveals the only way to defeat the tempting visions supplied by Satan and the world: by obedience to the will of God. It would be appropriate to discover how much we are willing to lose to share his obedience.

Music For Worship For First Sunday In Lent

NOTES	CYCLE A	CYCLE B	CYCLE C
	God The Father, Be Our Stay	Who Trusts In God, A Strong Abode	A Mighty Fortress Is Our God
	A Mighty Fortress Is Our God	Rise, O Children Of Salvation	God The Father, Be Our Stay
	In Adam We Have All Been One	In Thee Is Gladness	Lift Every Voice And Sing
	Praise And Thanks And Adoration	Lord, Thee I Love With All My Heart	Praise To The Lord, The Almighty
	Guide Me Ever, Great Redeemer	Jesus, Still Lead On	Where Charity And Love Prevail
	Lord, Keep Us Steadfast In Your Word	If God Himself Be For Me	God Loved The World
	Lord Of Our Life	God, My Lord, My Strength	Once He Came In Blessing
			All Who Would Valiant Be

Weekly Record

Date			
Entrance Hymn			
Hymn Of The Day			
Anthem/ Special Music			
Sermon Title			
Lay Reader			
Attendance			

Second Sunday In Lent

Readings

LESSON	CYCLE A	CYCLE B	CYCLE C
	Revised Common	**Revised Common**	**Revised Common**
First	Genesis 12:1-4a	Genesis 17:1-7, 15-16	Genesis 15:1-12, 17-18
Second	Romans 4:1-5, 13-17	Romans 4:13-25	Philippians 3:17—4:1
Gospel	John 3:1-17 or Matthew 17:1-9	Mark 8:31-38 or Mark 9:2-9	Luke 13:31-35 or Luke 9:28-36
	Episcopal	**Episcopal**	**Episcopal**
First	Genesis 12:1-8	Genesis 22:1-14	Genesis 15:1-12, 17-18
Second	Romans 4:1-5 (6-12), 13-17	Romans 8:31-39	Philippians 3:17—4:1
Gospel	John 3:1-17	Mark 8:31-38	Luke 13:(22-30) 31-35
	Lutheran	**Lutheran**	**Lutheran**
First	Genesis 12:1-8	Genesis 28:10-17 (18-22)	Jeremiah 26:8-15
Second	Romans 4:1-5, 13-17	Romans 5:1-11	Philippians 3:17—4:1
Gospel	John 4:5-26 (27-30, 39-42)	Mark 8:31-38	Luke 13:31-35
	Roman Catholic	**Roman Catholic**	**Roman Catholic**
First	Genesis 12:1-4	Genesis 22:1-2, 9-13, 15-18	Genesis 15:5-12, 17-18
Second	2 Timothy 1:8b-10	Romans 8:31-34	Philippians 3:17—4:1
Gospel	Matthew 17:1-9	Mark 9:2-10	Luke 9:28-36

Notes	Special Notes For A	Special Notes For B	Special Notes For C
Creed: Nicene **Color:** Purple **Special Notation:** Pick up the cross. Recognize this "I" has been put to death and that the new "I" may live freely, fully, powerfully.	The promise of salvation is given to Abraham. Also to a Samaritan woman, and to all of us, justified by grace through faith. Jesus introduces a new kind of worship, in spirit and in truth. Jesus announces, "I am the Messiah."	Jacob tried to reach God by ladder when all he had to do was become aware that God had come to him.	Jesus is a prophet and the world hates prophets. Prophets of our time are hated and attempts are made to destroy them. Recount the lives of saints who were killed while doing the work God set before them, i.e. Dietrich Bonhoeffer.

Music For Worship For Second Sunday In Lent

NOTES	CYCLE A	CYCLE B	CYCLE C
	Lord, Thee I Love With All My Heart	"Take Up Your Cross," The Savior Said	Jesus, Refuge Of The Weary
	"Take Up Your Cross," The Savior Said	Jesus, Refuge Of The Weary	Lord, Thee I Love With All My Heart
	O Jesus Christ, May Grateful Hymns Be Rising	How Blessed Is This Place, O Lord	O Jesus, Joy Of Loving Hearts
	Jesus, Refuge Of The Weary	Only-Begotten, Word Of God Eternal	"Take Up Your Cross," The Savior Said
		O God Of Jacob	
		One There Is Above All Others	
		O Christ, Our Hope	
		"Come, Follow Me," The Savior Spake	
		Let Us, Ever Walk With Jesus	
		Around You, O Lord Jesus	
		O God, My Faithful God	

Weekly Record

Date						
Entrance Hymn						
Hymn Of The Day						
Anthem/ Special Music						
Sermon Title						
Lay Reader						
Attendance						

Third Sunday In Lent

Readings

LESSON		CYCLE A	CYCLE B	CYCLE C
		Revised Common	**Revised Common**	**Revised Common**
First		Exodus 17:1-7	Exodus 20:1-17	Isaiah 55:1-9
Second		Romans 5:1-11	1 Corinthians 1:18-25	1 Corinthians 10:1-13
Gospel		John 4:5-42	John 2:13-22	Luke 13:1-9
		Episcopal	**Episcopal**	**Episcopal**
First		Exodus 17:1-7	Exodus 20:1-17	Exodus 3:1-15
Second		Romans 5:1-11	Romans 7:13-25	1 Corinthians 10:1-13
Gospel		John 4:5-26 (27-38) 39-42	John 2:13-22	Luke 13:1-9
		Lutheran	**Lutheran**	**Lutheran**
First		Isaiah 42:14-21	Exodus 20:1-17	Exodus 3:1-8b, 10-15
Second		Ephesians 5:8-14	1 Corinthians 1:22-25	1 Corinthians 10:1-13
Gospel		John 9:1-41 or John 9:13-17, 34-39	John 2:13-22	Luke 13:1-9
		Roman Catholic	**Roman Catholic**	**Roman Catholic**
First		Exodus 17:3-7	Exodus 20:1-17	Exodus 3:1-8
Second		Romans 5:1-2, 5-8	1 Corinthians 1:22-25	1 Corinthians 10:1-6, 10-12
Gospel		John 4:5-42	John 2:13-22	Luke 13:1-9

Notes

Creed: Nicene
Color: Purple
Special Notation: The cleansing of the temple; the promise of Jesus' resurrection.

Special Notes For A

Contrast between darkness and light. Darkness is spiritual death, hopelessness, separation. Light is life, a relationship with God. The one for whom Jesus creates new eyes not only can see what is there but can also see that Jesus is Lord. It is difficult for some to accept light, preferring darkness.

Special Notes For B

Recital of Torah story and proclamation of the Decalog provides sense of identity and code of ethics in any wilderness. The temple about to be torn down is his body-life and then in three days he will be raised again. Sunday school might do a mural of the 10 commandments.

Special Notes For C

Luke lays down hard terms for children of God. Judgment falls on all people. No one suffers disaster because he or she is more sinful than others. Our fruits reveal us. Temptation to idolatry is common to all. The gardener digs, cultivates and waits. Moses heard God say he would save his people. But we must all repent.

Music For Worship For Third Sunday In Lent

NOTES	CYCLE A	CYCLE B	CYCLE C
	May God Bestow On Us His Grace O God Of Earth And Altar Jesus, The Very Thought Of You In The Cross Of Christ I Glory	O God Of Earth And Altar In The Cross Of Christ I Glory Oh, That The Lord Would Guide My Ways Sing Praise To God, The Highest Good Your Word, O Lord, Is Gentle Dew	In The Cross Of Christ I Glory May God Bestow On Us This Grace God, Whose Almighty Word O God Of Earth And Altar

Weekly Record

Date			
Entrance Hymn			
Hymn Of The Day			
Anthem/ Special Music			
Sermon Title			
Lay Reader			
Attendance			

Fourth Sunday In Lent

Readings

LESSON		CYCLE A	CYCLE B	CYCLE C
		Revised Common	**Revised Common**	**Revised Common**
First		1 Samuel 16:1-13	Numbers 21:4-9	Joshua 5:9-12
Second		Ephesians 5:8-14	Ephesians 2:1-10	2 Corinthians 5:16-21
Gospel		John 9:1-41	John 3:14-21	Luke 15:1-3, 11b-32
		Episcopal	**Episcopal**	**Episcopal**
First		1 Samuel 16:1-13	2 Chronicles 36:14-23	Joshua (4:9-24); 5:9-12
Second		Ephesians 5:(1-7), 8-14	Ephesians 2:4-10	2 Corinthians 5:17-21
Gospel		John 9:1-13 (14-27) 28-38	John 3:14-21	Luke 15:11-32
		Lutheran	**Lutheran**	**Lutheran**
First		Hosea 5:15—6:2	Numbers 21:4-9	Isaiah 12:1-6
Second		Romans 8:1-10	Ephesians 2:4-10	1 Corinthians 1:8-31 or 1:18, 22-25
Gospel		Matthew 20:17-28	John 3:14-21	Luke 15:1-3, 11-32
		Roman Catholic	**Roman Catholic**	**Roman Catholic**
First		1 Samuel 16:1b, 6-7, 10-13	2 Chronicles 36:14-17, 19-23	Joshua 5:9-12
Second		Ephesians 5:8-14	Ephesians 2:4-10	2 Corinthians 5:17-21
Gospel		John 9:1-41	John 3:14-21	Luke 15:1-3, 11-32

Notes

Creed: Nicene
Color: Purple
Special Notation: God's love for the world to which the son came to bring light and judgment.

Special Notes For A

Lent should help us grow in Christ to the point where we can "boast of the Lord" not merely of our faithfulness in the busy work of the church.

Special Notes For B

Pilgrim people moan and complain about the uncertainties of their journey and their frailty of faith shows their misery about being left to die in the desert. God's judgment is a swift act of retribution against a puny faith, but he also provides a way of deliverance and life. A reading group could make complaints of people in contemporary wilderness to compare with those Moses heard long ago.

Special Notes For C

God's goodness is unconditional. An errant and repentant son has the same claim as the one who has faithfully tended the business of church life. He can join in the love and forgiveness by sharing in the feast. The worldwide crisis of racial, political and cultural tensions poses the question of whether or not we have rejoiced that the lost have returned.

Music For Worship For Fourth Sunday In Lent

NOTES

CYCLE A	CYCLE B	CYCLE C
I Trust, O Christ, In You Alone God Loved The World In Adam We Have All Been One On My Heart Imprint Your Image	On My Heart Imprint Your Image Amazing Grace, How Sweet The Sound Deep Were His Wounds O Christ, Our King, Creator, Lord Wide Open Are Your Hands Give To Our God Immortal Praise What Wondrous Love Is This	On My Heart Imprint Your Image God Love The World I Trust, O Christ, In You Alone Lord Of Glory, You Have Bought Us

Weekly Record

Date					
Entrance Hymn					
Hymn Of The Day					
Anthem/ Special Music					
Sermon Title					
Lay Reader					
Attendance					

Fifth Sunday In Lent

Readings

LESSON		CYCLE A	CYCLE B	CYCLE C
		Revised Common	**Revised Common**	**Revised Common**
First		Ezekiel 37:1-14	Jeremiah 31:31-34	Isaiah 43:16-21
Second		Romans 8:6-11	Hebrews 5:5-10	Philippians 3:4b-14
Gospel		John 11:1-45	John 12:20-33	John 12:1-8
		Episcopal	**Episcopal**	**Episcopal**
First		Ezekiel 37:1-3 (4-10), 11-14	Jeremiah 31:31-34	Isaiah 43:16-21
Second		Romans 6:16-23	Hebrews 5:(1-4) 5-10	Philippians 3:8-14
Gospel		John 11:(1-17) 18-44	John 12:20-33	Luke 20:9-19
		Lutheran	**Lutheran**	**Lutheran**
First		Ezekiel 37:1-3 (4-10), 11-14	Jeremiah 31:31-34	Isaiah 43:16-21
Second		Romans 8:11-19	Hebrews 5:7-9	Philippians 3:8-14
Gospel		John 11:1-53 or John 11:47-53	John 12:20-33	Luke 20:9-19
		Roman Catholic	**Roman Catholic**	**Roman Catholic**
First		Ezekiel 37:12-14	Jeremiah 31:31-34	Isaiah 43:16-21
Second		Romans 8:8-11	Hebrews 5:7-9	Philippians 3:8-14
Gospel		John 11:1-45	John 12:20-23	John 8:1-11

Notes	Special Notes For A	Special Notes For B	Special Notes For C
Cred: Nicene **Color:** Purple **Special Notation:** Jesus' moving toward his death and glorification; the call to die in order to live.	The impact of the lessons today is radical. As we are thinking of the cross, God's Word shouts about life. Lazarus is raised and the psalmist is rescued. "I am the resurrection and the life" Jesus declares and it is central to our faith.	Parable of wheat seeds — requires death and burial — the miracle of resurrection — the victorious sprouting of new life.	We hear of the judgment about to fall on those who reject the Son of God. The enemies resent the truth when it is spoken about them. Isaiah promises a new thing will be created by God.

Music For Worship For Fifth Sunday In Lent

NOTES	CYCLE A	CYCLE B	CYCLE C
	My Song Is Love Unknown Christ The Life Of All The Living Breathe On Me, Breath Of God Come, Thou Fount Of Every Blessing Let Us Ever Walk With Jesus Jesus, I Will Ponder Now Your Heart, O God, Is Grieved	Glory Be To Jesus Christ The Life Of All The Living To You, Omniscient Lord Of All Renew Me, O Eternal Light A Lamb Goes Uncomplaining Forth Now The Green Blade Rises My Heart Is Longing We Sing The Praise Of Him Who Died	My Song Is Love Unknown Christ The Life Of All The Living Kyrie, God, Father In Heav'n Above Beneath the Cross Of Jesus We Sing The Praise Of Him Who Died When I Survey The Wondrous Cross God Loved The World

Weekly Record

Date				
Entrance Hymn				
Hymn Of The Day				
Anthem/ Special Music				
Sermon Title				
Lay Reader				
Attendance				

Palm Sunday — Passion Sunday

Readings

LESSON	CYCLE A	CYCLE B	CYCLE C
	Revised Common	**Revised Common**	**Revised Common**
First	Isaiah 50:4-9a	Isaiah 50:4-9a	Isaiah 50:4-9a
Second	Philippians 2:5-11	Philippians 2:5-11	Philippians 2:5-11
Gospel	Matthew 27:11-54 or 26:14—27:66	Mark 14:1—15:47 or 15:1-39 (40-47)	Luke 22:14—23:56 or 23:1-49
	Episcopal	**Episcopal**	**Episcopal**
First	Isaiah 45:21-25 or 52:13—53:12	Isaiah 45:21-25 or 52:13—53:12	Isaiah 45:21-25 or 52:13—53:12
Second	Philippians 2:5-11	Philippians 2:5-11	Philippians 2:5-11
Gospel	Matthew (26:36-75) 27:1-54 (55-66)	Mark 11:1-11a; 14:32-72; 15:1-39 (40-47)	Luke (22:37-71) 23:1-49 (50-56)
	Lutheran	**Lutheran**	**Lutheran**
First	Isaiah 50:4-9a	Zechariah 9:9-10	Deuteronomy 32:36-39
Second	Philippians 2:5-11	Philippians 2:5-11	Philippians 2:5-11
Gospel	Matthew 26:1—27:66 or 27:11-54	Mark 11:1-10; 14:1—15:47	Luke 22:1—23:56 or 23:1-49
	Roman Catholic	**Roman Catholic**	**Roman Catholic**
First	Isaiah 50:4-7	Isaiah 50:4-7	Isaiah 50:4-7
Second	Philippians 2:6-11	Philippians 2:6-11	Philippians 2:6-11
Gospel	Matthew 26:14—27:66	Mark 14:1—15:47	Luke 22:14—23:56

Notes	Special Notes For A	Special Notes For B	Special Notes For C
Creed: Apostles' **Color:** Red **Special Notation:** The final events of Jesus' life.	We start the day with a procession of palms and shouts of Hosanna. Today's story is about the servant Isaiah spoke of, the obedient one Paul spoke of, abandoned on the cross dying for the sins of the people. It is as if Jesus is in charge, engineering the cross. We end the day in total silence. The transition from joy to quiet is powerful.	A group might read "The Passion of Our Lord According to Mark," a history for several voices. Procession with palm from outside or narthex. If entire passion is read, sermon may be brief devotional commentary.	The theme continues in the coalition of Jesus' enemies, his abandonment even by his disciples and the irresistable progress of the Son of Man fulfilling his mission in obedience to the Father. The strange mixture of humility and triumph, glory and suffering, power and vulnerability keynotes the rest of Holy Week.

Music For Worship For Palm Sunday — Passion Sunday

NOTES

CYCLE A	CYCLE B	CYCLE C
The Royal Banners Forward Go O Sacred Head, Now Wounded	The Royal Banners Forward Go O Sacred Head, Now Wounded Beneath The Cross Of Jesus O Christ, Our King, Creator, Lord It Happened That Fateful Night	The Royal Banners Forward Go O Sacred Head, Now Wounded

Weekly Record

Date					
Entrance Hymn					
Hymn Of The Day					
Anthem/ Special Music					
Sermon Title					
Lay Reader					
Attendance					

Maundy Thursday

Readings

LESSON	CYCLE A	CYCLE B	CYCLE C
	Revised Common	**Revised Common**	**Revised Common**
First	Exodus 12:1-4 (5-10) 11-14	Exodus 12:1-4 (5-10) 11-14	Exodus 12:1-4 (5-10) 11-14
Second	1 Corinthians 11:23-26	1 Corinthians 11:23-26	1 Corinthians 11:23-26
Gospel	John 13:1-17, 31b-35	John 13:1-17, 31b-35	John 13:1-17, 31b-35
	Episcopal	**Episcopal**	**Episcopal**
First	Exodus 12:1-14a	Exodus 12:1-14a	Exodus 12:1-14a
Second	1 Corinthians 11:23-26 (27-32)	1 Corinthians 11:23-26 (27-32)	1 Corinthians 11:23-26 (27-32)
Gospel	John 13:1-15 or Luke 22:14-30	John 13:1-15 or Luke 22:14-30	John 13:1-15 or Luke 22:14-30
	Lutheran	**Lutheran**	**Lutheran**
First	Exodus 12:1-14	Exodus 24:3-11	Jeremiah 31:31-34
Second	1 Corinthians 11:17-32	1 Corinthians 10:16-17 (18-21)	Hebrews 10:15-19
Gospel	John 13:1-17, 34	Mark 14:12-26	Luke 22:7-20
	Roman Catholic	**Roman Catholic**	**Roman Catholic**
First	Exodus 12:1-8, 11-14	Exodus 12:1-8, 11-14	Exodus 12:1-8, 11-14
Second	1 Corinthians 11:23-26	1 Corinthians 11:23-26	1 Corinthians 11:23-26
Gospel	John 13:1-15	John 13:1-15	John 13:1-15

Notes

Creed: Apostles'
Color: Red
Special Notation: Maundy means "commandment." Jesus offers a new commandment.

Special Notes For A

God's faithful gather to commemorate the day when Christ instituted the meal of the new covenant. As we meet for forgiveness and celebration, we have no difficulty discerning the body of the church. We belong to each other. At the close of liturgy the altar is stripped in preparation for Good Friday and we walk away in silence even as Jesus walked into the garden of Gethsemane.

Special Notes For B

John 13:1-17, 34 is used if observing washing of feet. God's grace is revealed therein. A youth, middle-aged and elderly persons, one or two being female, to be selected. Pitcher, basin, water and towel provided with apron for minister.

Special Notes For C

This is the day of reconciliation, the day in which the discipline of penitence began on Ash Wednesday is resolved in the mercies of God.

Music For Worship For Maundy Thursday

NOTES	CYCLE A	CYCLE B	CYCLE C
	We Who Once Were Dead O Lord, We Praise You Thee We Adore, O Hidden Savior Where Charity And Love Prevail	We Who Once Were Dead Thee We Adore, O Hidden Savior Of The Glorious Body Telling It Happened On The Fateful Night	We Who Once Were Dead Love Consecrates The Humblest Act Thee We Adore, O Hidden Savior Lord Jesus Christ, You Have Prepared Around You, O Lord Jesus

Weekly Record

Date						
Entrance Hymn						
Hymn Of The Day						
Anthem/ Special Music						
Sermon Title						
Lay Reader						
Attendance						

Good Friday

LESSON	CYCLE A	CYCLE B	CYCLE C
	Revised Common	**Revised Common**	**Revised Common**
First	Isaiah 52:13—53:12	Isaiah 52:13—53:12	Isaiah 52:13—53:12
Second	Hebrews 10:16-25	Hebrews 10:16-25	Hebrews 10:16-25
Gospel	John 18:1—19:42	John 18:1—19:42	John 18:1—19:42
	Episcopal	**Episcopal**	**Episcopal**
First	Isaiah 52:13—53:12 or Genesis 22:1-18	Isaiah 52:13—53:12 or Genesis 22:1-18	Isaiah 52:13—53:12 or Genesis 22:1-18
Second	Hebrews 10:1-25	Hebrews 10:1-25	Hebrews 10:1-25
Gospel	John (18:1-40) 19:1-37	John (18:1-40) 19:1-37	John (18:1-40) 19:1-37
	Lutheran	**Lutheran**	**Lutheran**
First	Isaiah 52:13—53:12	Isaiah 52:13:53:12	Isaiah 52:13—53:12
Second	Hebrews 4:14-16; 5;7-9	Hebrews 4:14-16; 5:7-9	Hebrews 4:14-16; 5:7-9
Gospel	John 18:1—19:42	John 18:1—19:42	John 18:1—19:42
	Roman Catholic	**Roman Catholic**	**Roman Catholic**
First	Isaiah 52:13—53:12	Isaiah 52:13—53:12	Isaiah 52:13—53:12
Second	Hebrews 4:14-16; 5;7-9	Hebrews 4:14-16; 5:7-9	Hebrews 4:14-16; 5:7-9
Gospel	John 18:1—19:42	John 18:1—19:42	John 18:1—19:42

Notes	Special Notes For A	Special Notes For B	Special Notes For C
Creed: Apostles' **Color:** Black **Special Notation:** The events surrounding the last hours of Jesus' life.	"King of the Jews" is a sign in mockery. He is pierced in hands and feet, dying and abandoned. His appearance is so marred and his ministry so rejected that the people he came to save turn away. And yet, there is a prediction of praise.	People should enter and leave church in silence but may remain for prayer and meditation. Most appropriately held near 3 p.m., traditional hour of Jesus' death. Large, rough-hewn wooden cross used. Offerings received at entrance to church only. No opening hymn. Creed is not used.	The final sacrifice of Christ reveals his final victory. Everything Isaiah said about the suffering servant came true. Here is a glimpse into the working of God's history through the redemptive life and death of his Son. Jesus knew, understood and controlled these events in a way lost to those who thought they were shaping his destiny.

Music For Worship For Good Friday

NOTES

CYCLE A	CYCLE B	CYCLE C
Deep Were His Wounds	Deep Were His Wounds	Deep Were His Wounds
O Sacred Head Now Wounded	O Sacred Head Now Wounded	O Sacred Head Now Wounded
Lamb Of God, Pure And Sinless	Sing, My Tongue	At The Cross, Her Station Keeping
Ah, Holy Jesus	Were You There	Jesus, In Thy Dying Woes
The Royal Banners Forward Go	In The Hour Of Trial	There Is A Green Hill Far Away
	Go To Dark Gethsemane	

Weekly Record

Date				
Entrance Hymn				
Hymn Of The Day				
Anthem/ Special Music				
Sermon Title				
Lay Reader				
Attendance				

Easter Sunday

Readings

LESSON	CYCLE A	CYCLE B	CYCLE C
	Revised Common	**Revised Common**	**Revised Common**
First	Acts 10:34-43	Acts 10:34-43	Acts 10:34-43
Second	Colossians 3;1-4	Corinthians 15:1-11	1 Corinthians 15:19-26
Gospel	John 20:1-18	John 20:1-18	John 20:1-18
	Episcopal	**Episcopal**	**Episcopal**
First	Acts 10:34-43	Acts 10:34-43	Acts 10:34-43
Second	Colossians 3:1-4	Colossians 3:1-4	Colossians 3:1-4
Gospel	John 20:1-10 (11-18)	Mark 16:1-8	Luke 24:1-10
	Lutheran	**Lutheran**	**Lutheran**
First	Acts 10:34-43	Isaiah 25:6-9	Exodus 15:1-11
Second	Colossians 3:1-4	1 Corinthians 15:19-28	1 Corinthians 15:1-11
Gospel	John 20:1-9 (10-18)	Mark 16:1-8	Luke 24:1-11
	Roman Catholic	**Roman Catholic**	**Roman Catholic**
First	Acts 10:34, 37-43	Acts 10:34-43	Acts 10:34, 37-43
Second	1 Corinthians 3:1-4	Colossians 3:1-4	Colossians 3:1-4
Gospel	John 20:1-9	John 20:1-9	John 20:1-9

Notes

Creed: Nicene
Color: White or gold
Special Notation: Fulfillment of God's promises. Our silent fear as we look into the empty tomb becomes wonder and joy as we realize that he is risen.

Special Notes For A

The tragedy of the tomb suddenly becomes a shocking revelation: "He is not here; for he has risen!" How awesome is the gradual penetration of the stunning truth: "You have been raised with Christ; seek the things that are above."

Special Notes For B

Processional and recessional with cross, banner, crucifer, choir and the Word in our midst. Decorate with tulips and small bells.

Special Notes For C

Try to imagine the expectations of the women who went to the tomb. Then the shock of what they found and heard from the beings present there. Recognizing Jesus then changed from physical faculties to remembering his words. It took time for the disciples to adapt to that recognition.

Music For Worship For Easter Sunday

NOTES	CYCLE A	CYCLE B	CYCLE C
	Good Christian Friends, Rejoice And Sing At The Lamb's High Feast We Sing Alleluia! Sing To Jesus Come, Risen Lord Hosanna To The Living Lord I Know That My Redeemer Lives Jesus Christ, My Sure Defense O Christ, Our Hope	Christians, To The Paschal Victim Good Christian Friends, Rejoice And Sing Jesus Christ Is Risen Today Look, Now He Stands Alleluia! Sing To Jesus At The Lamb's High Feast We Sing Come, Risen Lord Hosanna To The Living Lord Christ, Our Hope Jesus Christ, My Sure Defense I Know That My Redeemer Lives	Good Christian Friends, Rejoice And Sing At The Lamb's High Feast We Sing Alleluia! Sing To Jesus Come, Risen Lord Hosanna To The Living Lord O Christ, Our Hope Jesus Christ, My Sure Defense

Weekly Record

Date			
Entrance Hymn			
Hymn Of The Day			
Anthem/ Special Music			
Sermon Title			
Lay Reader			
Attendance			

Second Sunday Of Easter

Readings

LESSON	CYCLE A	CYCLE B	CYCLE C
	Revised Common	**Revised Common**	**Revised Common**
First	Acts 2:14a, 22-32	Acts 4:32-35	Acts 5:27-32
Second	1 Peter 1:3-9	1 John 1:1—2:2	Revelation 1:4-8
Gospel	John 20:19-31	John 20:19-31	John 20:19-31
	Episcopal	**Episcopal**	**Episcopal**
First	Acts 2:14a, 22-32	Acts 3:12a, 13-15	Acts 5:12a, 17-22, 25-29
Second	1 Peter 1:3-9	1 John 5:1-6	Revelation 1:(1-8) 9-19
Gospel	John 20:19-31	John 20:19-31	John 20:19-31
	Lutheran	**Lutheran**	**Lutheran**
First	Acts 2:14a, 22-32	Acts 3:13-15, 17-26	Acts 5:12, 17-32
Second	1 Peter 1:3-9	1 John 5:1-6	Revelation 1:4-18
Gospel	John 20:19-31	John 20:19-31	John 20:19-31
	Roman Catholic	**Roman Catholic**	**Roman Catholic**
First	Acts 2:42-47	Acts 4:32-35	Acts 5:12-16
Second	1 Peter 1:3-9	1 John 5:1-6	Revelation 1:9-11a, 12-13, 17-19
Gospel	John 20:19-31	John 20:19-31	John 20:19-31

Notes

Creed: Nicene

Color: White

Special Notation: Doubt is overcome by Christ's appearance in our lives. He will appear again and again so that we too may see and in seeing believe.

Special Notes For A

Thomas needs proof positive in order to believe. Since that would not be given to anyone else, Jesus blessed future generations who would believe without seeing. The inheritance noted in the second lesson is the gathering point and the gift of hope from God, the Father.

Special Notes For B

Have any ever denied the Lord? Many will say, "never!" But these are denials of omission as well as commission. Truth and faith bear witness. We are not granted physical proof as was Thomas, but if we have received the Spirit, we believe. As believers, we should be alert to the casual breaking of the commandments.

Special Notes For C

About a week after the resurrection, all disciples except the absent Thomas, were convinced of the reality of Jesus' resurrection. The most convincing evidence was the peace he brought and the mission he sought for them. Thomas needed touch as well as sight and hearing. But it brought him belief. Jesus then blessed those who would "recognize" him without that physical need.

Music For Worship For Second Sunday Of Easter

NOTES	CYCLE A	CYCLE B	CYCLE C
	Come, You Faithful, Raise The Strain That Easter Day With Joy Was Bright O Sons And Daughters Of The King Christ Is Risen! Alleluia! The First Day Of The Week Awake, My Heart, With Gladness Jesus Lives! The Victory's Won! Make Songs Of Joy A Savior, Precious Savior	Come, You Faithful, Raise The Strain That Easter Day With Joy Was Bright Praise The Lord Of Heaven Ye Watchers And Ye Holy Ones Let The Whole Creation Cry All Creatures Of Our God And King	Come, You Faithful! Raise The Strain That Easter Day With Joy Was Bright Look, The Sight Is Glorious The Head That Once Was Crowned

Weekly Record

Date			
Entrance Hymn			
Hymn Of The Day			
Anthem/ Special Music			
Sermon Title			
Lay Reader			
Attendance			

Third Sunday Of Easter

Readings

LESSON		CYCLE A	CYCLE B	CYCLE C
First Second Gospel		**Revised Common** Acts 2:14a, 36-41 1 Peter 1:17-23 Luke 24:13-35	**Revised Common** Acts 3:12-19 1 John 3:1-7 Luke 24:36b-48	**Revised Common** Acts 9:1-6 (7-20) Revelation 5:11-14 John 21:1-19
First Second Gospel		**Episcopal** Acts 2:14a, 36-47 1 Peter 1:17-23 Luke 24:13-35	**Episcopal** Acts 4:5-12 1 John 1:1—2:2 Luke 24:36b-48	**Episcopal** Acts 9:1-19a Revelation 5:6-14 John 21:1-14
First Second Gospel		**Lutheran** Acts 2:14a, 36-47 1 Peter 1:17-21 Luke 24:13-35	**Lutheran** Acts 4:8-12 1 John 1:1—2:2 Luke 24:36-49	**Lutheran** Acts 9:1-20 Revelation 5:11-14 John 21:1-14
First Second Gospel		**Roman Catholic** Acts 2:14, 22-28 1 Peter 1:17-21 Luke 24:13-35	**Roman Catholic** Acts 3:13-15, 17-19 1 John 2:1-5 Luke 23:36-48	**Roman Catholic** Acts 5:27b-32, 40b-41 Revelation 5:11-14 John 21:1-19
Notes		**Special Notes For A**	**Special Notes For B**	**Special Notes For C**
Creed: Nicene **Color:** White **Special Notation:** Doubting and in need of forgiveness, we are to repent and believe that Jesus is our risen Lord.		We must not forget the cost of our redemption. Martin Luther's meaning to the Second Article of the Apostles' Creed echoes the second lesson.	If any good is done through us, we must hasten to point out that Jesus Christ has accomplished it, not ourselves, as we are only instruments of his will. All power comes from on high and there is nothing that power cannot do.	The disciples have returned home to Galilee. They did not yet understand the presence and power of the risen Christ, but they knew he was with them. Children could make "fish prints."

NOTES	CYCLE A	CYCLE B	CYCLE C
	With High Delight Let Us Unite Now All The Vault Of Heaven Resounds When All Your Mercies, O My God For In Thy Name, O Lord, I Go May We Your Precepts, Lord, Fulfill Come, Risen Lord Abide With Us, Our Savior This Joyful Eastertide	Now All The Vault Of Heaven Resounds Look, Now He Stands Praise The Savior, Now And Ever Jesus Christ, My Sure Defense Wondrous Are Your Ways Of God! Here, O My Lord, I See Thee O Lord Of Light, Who Made The Stars O Christ, Our Hope He Is Arisen! Glorious Word!	With High Delight Let Us Unite Now All The Vault Of Heaven Resounds

Weekly Record

Date						
Entrance Hymn						
Hymn Of The Day						
Anthem/ Special Music						
Sermon Title						
Lay Reader						
Attendance						

Fourth Sunday Of Easter

Readings

LESSON	CYCLE A	CYCLE B	CYCLE C
	Revised Common	**Revised Common**	**Revised Common**
First	Acts 2:42-47	Acts 4:5-12	Acts 9:36-43
Second	1 Peter 2:19-25	1 John 3:16-24	Revelation 7:9-17
Gospel	John 10:1-10	John 10:11-18	John 10:22-30
	Episcopal	**Episcopal**	**Episcopal**
First	Acts 6:1-9; 7:2a, 51-60	Acts 4:(23-31) 32-37	Acts 13:15-16, 26-33 (34-39)
Second	1 Peter 2:19-25	1 John 1:3-8	Revelation 7:9-17
Gospel	John 10:1-10	John 10:11-16	John 10:22-30
	Lutheran	**Lutheran**	**Lutheran**
First	Acts 6:1-9; 7:2a, 51-60	Acts 4:23-33	Acts 13:15-16a, 26-33
Second	1 Peter 2:19-25	1 John 3:1-2	Revelation 7:9-17
Gospel	John 10:1-10	John 10:11-18	John 10:22-30
	Roman Catholic	**Roman Catholic**	**Roman Catholic**
First	Acts 2:14a, 36-41	Acts 4:8-12	Acts 13:14, 43-52
Second	1 Peter 2:20b-25	1 John 3:1-2	Revelation 7:9, 14b-17
Gospel	John 10:1-10	John 10:11-18	John 10:27-30

Notes

Creed: Nicene
Color: White
Special Notation: We often feel alienated and trapped by the powers of the world. Jesus, as our loving shepherd, will not desert us.

Special Notes For A

Believers must use discernment. People are not always what they profess to be. But living should not be done in hiding or in refusing to be involved. Sometimes religious leaders make Christianity too easy.

Special Notes For B

The love God has for us, his children, is great indeed. We know this because he sent his Son, the Christ, to suffer and die in our place, so we would not be scattered and lost to him forever. Who are the other sheep he must bring also? Are we tuned in to the Shepherd's voice?

Special Notes For C

The metaphor of sheep recognizing the shepherd by his voice prepared the disciples for listening to his voice. The result of this hearing and following is protection from the enemy, death. Sheep and shepherd craft projects suitable for children.

Music For Worship For Fourth Sunday Of Easter

NOTES	CYCLE A	CYCLE B	CYCLE C
	O God Of Jacob The Lord's My Shepherd Savior, Like A Shepherd Lead Us I Know That My Redeemer Lives	Praise The Lord, Rise Up Rejoicing I know That My Redeemer Lives The Lord's My Shepherd O God Of Jacob	O God Of Jacob The King Of Love My Shepherd Is The Lord's My Shepherd I Know That My Redeemer Lives

Weekly Record

Date			
Entrance Hymn			
Hymn Of The Day			
Anthem/ Special Music			
Sermon Title			
Lay Reader			
Attendance			

Fifth Sunday Of Easter

Readings

LESSON	CYCLE A	CYCLE B	CYCLE C
	Revised Common	**Revised Common**	**Revised Common**
First	Acts 7:55-60	Acts 8:26-40	Acts 11:1-8
Second	1 Peter 2:2-10	1 John 4:7-21	Revelation 21:1-6
Gospel	John 14:1-14	John 15:1-8	John 13:31-35
	Episcopal	**Episcopal**	**Episcopal**
First	Acts 17:1-15	Acts 8:26-40	Acts 13:44-52
Second	1 Peter 2:1-10	1 John 3 (14-17) 18-24	Revelation 19:1, 4-9
Gospel	John 14:1-14	John 14:15-21	John 13:31-35
	Lutheran	**Lutheran**	**Lutheran**
First	Acts 17:1-15	Acts 8:26-40	Acts 13:44-52
Second	1 Peter 2:4-10	1 John 3:18-24	Revelation 21:1-5
Gospel	John 14:1-12	John 15:1-8	John 13:31-35
	Roman Catholic	**Roman Catholic**	**Roman Catholic**
First	Acts 6:1-7	Acts 9:25-31	Acts 14:21-27
Second	1 Peter 2:4-9	1 John 3:18-24	Revelation 21:1-5a
Gospel	John 14:1-12	John 15:1-8	John 13:31-33a, 34-35

Notes

Creed: Nicene
Color: White
Special Notation: Jesus calls us to abide in him and his disciples. We are to love one another and bear fruits of the Spirit.

Special Notes For A

Jesus was getting ready to leave and those who loved him were confused and hurt. He was entrusting them with an important and difficult job. His answer to their anxiety was "Believe in me."

Special Notes For B

When reading scriptures, people often fail to understand their meaning. So it was with the eunuch of Ethiopia. The Spirit caused Philip to approach him and begin to teach. When the eunuch was enlightened, he asked to be baptized. Then Philip went on his way to preach elsewhere, and the eunuch took the good news back home with him.

Special Notes For C

Jesus is revealing to his disciples that they were called to carry on his mission and messages. He prepared them for his leaving. His presence would henceforth be of a different dimension. He gave it as a new commandment.

Music For Worship For Fifth Sunday Of Easter

NOTES	CYCLE A	CYCLE B	CYCLE C
	At The Lamb's High Feast We Sing Amid The World's Bleak Wilderness Lord Of All Nations Grant Me Grace Jesus, Thy Boundless Love To Me	Jesus Lives! The Victory's Won Jesus, Thy Boundless Love To Me Amid The World's Bleak Wilderness We Know That Christ Is Raised God Of Our Life, All-Glorious Lord To God The Holy Spirit Let Us Pray Eternal Spirit Of The Living Christ Come Down, O Love Divine Chief Of Sinners Though I Be	At The Lamb's High Feast We Sing You Are The Way Amid The World's Bleak Wilderness Jesus, Thy Boundless Love To Me

Weekly Record

Date			
Entrance Hymn			
Hymn Of The Day			
Anthem/ Special Music			
Sermon Title			
Lay Reader			
Attendance			

Sixth Sunday Of Easter

Readings

LESSON	CYCLE A	CYCLE B	CYCLE C
	Revised Common	**Revised Common**	**Revised Common**
First	Acts 17:22-31	Acts 10:44-48	Acts 16:9-15
Second	1 Peter 3:13-22	1 John 5:1-6	Revelation 21:10; 21:22—22:5
Gospel	John 14:15-21	John 15:9-17	John 14:23-29
	Episcopal	**Episcopal**	**Episcopal**
First	Acts 17:22-31	Acts 11:19-30	Acts 14:8-18
Second	1 Peter 3:8-18	1 John 4:7-21	Revelation 21:22—22:5
Gospel	John 15:1-8	John 15:9-17	John 14:23-29
	Lutheran	**Lutheran**	**Lutheran**
First	Acts 17:22-31	Acts 11:19-30	Acts 14:8-18
Second	1 Peter 3:15-22	1 John 4:1-11	Revelation 21:10-14, 22-23
Gospel	John 14:15-21	John 15:9-17	John 14:23-29
	Roman Catholic	**Roman Catholic**	**Roman Catholic**
First	Acts 8:5-8, 14-17	Acts 10:25-26, 34-35, 44-48	Acts 15:1-2, 22-29
Second	1 Peter 3:15-18	1 John 4:7-10	Revelation 21:10-14, 22-23
Gospel	John 14:15-21	John 15:9-17	John 14:23-29

Notes	Special Notes For A	Special Notes For B	Special Notes For C
Cred: Nicene **Color:** White **Special Notation:** We belong to God so we are charged, as children, to love one another as we have been loved.	Reverence of Christ needs to be reflected in keeping his commandments. If one must suffer, it's better to suffer for upholding God's justice and righteousness. The Holy Spirit is our Counselor, assuring us of a continued relationship with Jesus.	Many went forth and traveled far preaching the Lord Jesus, for the Spirit was with them. There are false prophets in and of the world. They are not of God if they do not confess that Jesus came in the flesh, but are, rather, spirits of the antichrist. Jesus no longer calls us servants, but friends, because he has revealed the Father, in whom he is and who is in him.	Love and peace are continuing themes, as they are evidence of his presence. The Holy Spirit was also promised, who enabled the disciples to bring the love, the peace and God's Word and meal in their mission. Musical arts associated with this day. A choir festival, hymn sing or other musical service would be appropriate for this afternoon or evening. Might commemorate Durer's and Michelangelo's artistic contributions, too.

Music For Worship For Sixth Sunday Of Easter

NOTES	CYCLE A	CYCLE B	CYCLE C
	Dear Christians, One And All One There Is, Above All Others Welcome, Happy Morning! All Glory Be To God On High Eternal God, Before Your Throne Come, Oh, Come, O Quickening Spirit Come Down, O Love Divine Earth And All Stars! When In Our Music God Is Glorified Oh, Praise The Lord, My Son! How Marvelous God's Greatness	Now The Green Blade Rises One There Is, Above All Others Son Of God, Eternal Savior Lord Of All Nations, Grant Me Grace	Dear Christians, One And All One There Is, Above All Others

Weekly Record

Date			
Entrance Hymn			
Hymn Of The Day			
Anthem/ Special Music			
Sermon Title			
Lay Reader			
Attendance			

Ascension Of Our Lord

Readings

LESSON	CYCLE A	CYCLE B	CYCLE C
	Revised Common	**Revised Common**	**Revised Common**
First	Acts 1:1-11	Acts 1:1-11	Acts 1:1-11
Second	Ephesians 1:15-23	Ephesians 1:15-23	Ephesians 1:15-23
Gospel	Luke 24:44-53	Luke 24:44-53	Luke 24:44-53
	Episcopal	**Episcopal**	**Episcopal**
First	Acts 1:1-11	Acts 1:1-11	Acts 1:1-11
Second	Ephesians 1:15-23	Ephesians 1:15-23	Ephesians 1:15-23
Gospel	Luke 24:49-53	Luke 24:49-53	Luke 24:49-53
	Lutheran	**Lutheran**	**Lutheran**
First	Acts 1:1-11	Acts 1:1-11	Acts 1:1-11
Second	Ephesians 1:16-23	Ephesians 1:16-23	Ephesians 1:16-23
Gospel	Luke 24:44-53	Luke 24:44-53	Luke 24:44-53
	Roman Catholic	**Roman Catholic**	**Roman Catholic**
First	Acts 1:1-11	Acts 1:1-11	Acts 1:1-11
Second	Ephesians 1:17-23	Ephesians 1:17-23	Ephesians 1:17-22
Gospel	Matthew 28:16-20	Mark 16:15-20	Luke 24:46-53

Notes

Creed: Nicene
Color: White
Special Notation: He has broken all boundaries of time and space. Now his body is the church.

Special Notes For A

Jesus who put himself in his Father's hands at death, now is exalted "to the highest places above." The disciples carried his final blessing and his promise of the Spirit back to Jerusalem.

Special Notes For B

Paschal candle extinguished at reading of gospel as a sign of the end of appearances of the risen Jesus.

Special Notes For C

At reading of gospel words "He parted from them and was carried up into heaven" the Paschal candle is extinguished. Place candle near baptismal font and relight it for each baptism, reassuring all that Christ is alive and bestows life on all who are baptized. This service might terminate outside on a hill.

NOTES

CYCLE A	CYCLE B	CYCLE C
Up Through Endless Ranks Of Angels Lord, Enthroned In Heavenly Splendor Alleluia! Sing To Jesus A Hymn Of Glory Let Us Sing!	A Hymn Of Glory Let Us Sing! Crown Him With Many Crowns Rejoice, The Lord Is King! Lord, Enthroned In Heavenly Splendor At The Name Of Jesus O Christ, Our Hope And Have The Bright Immensities O God Of God, O Light Of Light	Up Through Endless Ranks Of Angels Look, The Sight Is Glorious Lord, Enthroned In Heavenly Splendor A Hymn Of Glory Let Us Sing! And Have The Bright Immensities At The Name Of Jesus Crown Him With Many Crowns

Weekly Record

Date				
Entrance Hymn				
Hymn Of The Day				
Anthem/ Special Music				
Sermon Title				
Lay Reader				
Attendance				

Seventh Sunday Of Easter

Readings

LESSON	CYCLE A	CYCLE B	CYCLE C
	Revised Common	**Revised Common**	**Revised Common**
First	Acts 1:6-14	Acts 1:15-17, 21-26	Acts 16:16-34
Second	1 Peter 4:12-14; 5:6-11	1 John 5:9-13	Revelation 22:12-14, 16-17, 20-21
Gospel	John 17:1-11	John 17:6-19	John 17:20-26
	Episcopal	**Episcopal**	**Episcopal**
First	Acts 1:(17) 8-14	Acts 1:15-26	Acts 16:16-34
Second	1 Peter 4:12-19	1 John 5:9-15	Revelation 22:12-14
Gospel	John 17:1-11	John 17:11b-19	John 17:20-26
	Lutheran	**Lutheran**	**Lutheran**
First	Acts 1:(1-7) 8-14	Acts 1:15-26	Acts 16:6-10
Second	1 Peter 4:12-17; 5:6-11	1 John 4:13-21	Revelation 22:12-17, 20
Gospel	John 17:1-11	John 17:11b-19	John 17:20-26
	Roman Catholic	**Roman Catholic**	**Roman Catholic**
First	Acts 1:12-14	Acts 1:15-17, 20-26	Acts 7:55—8:1a
Second	1 Peter 4:13-16	1 John 4:11-16	Revelation 22:12-14, 16-17, 20
Gospel	John 17:1-11a	John 17:11-19	John 17:20-26

Notes

Creed: Nicene
Color: White
Special Notation: The world encroaches on Christ's followers, but their coming empowerment and consecration will protect them as they spread the Word that that he is risen.

Special Notes For A

Jesus prays for his disciples who remain in the world "that they may be one." An excellent time for an ecumenical service. Pastor may invite congregation to join hands for the gospel reading or at least the final verse.

Special Notes For B

Bibles to grade four children. Jerusalem crosses to acolytes having served two years.

Special Notes For C

Hopefully, the steps we are taking in Christian unity will help in the recognition of the presence of the risen Lord. Ask congregation to join hands for the Lord's Prayer.

Music For Worship For Seventh Sunday Of Easter

NOTES	CYCLE A	CYCLE B	CYCLE C
	Oh, Love, How Deep	Have No Fear Little Flock	Oh, Love, How Deep
	Have No Fear, Little Flock	By All Your Saints In Warfare	Lord, Teach Us How To Pray Aright
	Lord, Receive This Company	O Christ, You Are The Light And Day	Have No Fear, Little Flock
	Crown Him With Many Crowns	Lord, Thee I Love With All My Heart	
	O Christ, Our Hope	I Trust, O Christ, In You Alone	
	Hail Thee, Festival Day	We Worship You, O God Of Night	
	A Hymn Of Glory Let Us Sing!		
	Up Through Endless Ranks Of Angels		
	And Have The Bright Immensities		

Weekly Record

Date					
Entrance Hymn					
Hymn Of The Day					
Anthem/ Special Music					
Sermon Title					
Lay Reader					
Attendance					

Day Of Pentecost

Readings

LESSON	CYCLE A	CYCLE B	CYCLE C
	Revised Common	**Revised Common**	**Revised Common**
First	Acts 2:1-21	Acts 2:1-21	Acts 2:1-21
Second	1 Corinthians 12:3b-13	Romans 8:22-27	Romans 8:14-17
Gospel	John 7:37-39	John 15:26-27; 16:4b-15	John 14:8-17 (25-27)
	Episcopal	**Episcopal**	**Episcopal**
First	Acts 2:1-11	Acts 2:1-11	Acts 2:1-11
Second	1 Corinthians 12:4-13	1 Corinthians 12:4-13	1 Corinthians 12:4-13
Gospel	John 20:19-23	John 20:19-23	John 20:19-23
	Lutheran	**Lutheran**	**Lutheran**
First	Joel 2:28-29	Ezekiel 37:1-14	Genesis 11:1-9
Second	Acts 2:1-21	Acts 2:1-21	Acts 2:1-21
Gospel	John 20:19-23	John 7:37-39a	John 15:26-27; 16:4b-11
	Roman Catholic	**Roman Catholic**	**Roman Catholic**
First	Acts 2:1-11	Acts 2:1-11	Acts 2:1-11
Second	1 Corinthians 12:3b-7, 12-13	1 Corinthians 12:3-7, 12-13	1 Corinthians 12:3b-7, 12-13
Gospel	John 20:19-23	John 20:19-23	John 20:19-23

Notes

Creed: Nicene

Color: Red

Special Notation: God again breathes the breath of life into the world, this time through the Spirit.

Special Notes For A

Commemoration of the descent of the Holy Spirit upon apostles and disciples who became a church in mission. It is the event that gave wings to the Easter victory. The spectator's reaction is "They are filled with new wine." This "new wine" is really that of which dreams and visions and incredible happenings are made.

Special Notes For B

Verse: Alleluia. Come, Holy Spirit, fill the hearts of your faithful people; set them on fire with your love. Alleluia. Several readers could speak text in different languages. The understood language (English) should be slower, louder and in the middle of the congregation. Processional mobile of red flames could be constructed. Red roses are fitting in altar flowers.

Special Notes For C

The culmination of Easter. The risen and ascended Christ sent the promised Spirit to the expectant church. The Spirit gives the church the necessary power and gifts to carry forth the glad news of the resurrection. "Christ is risen" could be spoken in different languages. Wind instruments have an obvious connection this day. This service could end outside indicating "the time for the work of the kingdom has begun."

Music For Worship For Day Of Pentecost

NOTES	CYCLE A	CYCLE B	CYCLE C
	To God The Holy Spirit Let Us Pray Come, Holy Ghost, God, And Lord Filled With The Spirit's Power Lord God, The Holy Ghost	Lord, God, The Holy Ghost Creator Spirit, Heavenly Dove Spirit Of God, Sent From Heaven Abroad To God The Holy Spirit Let Us Pray Spirit Of God, Unleashed On Earth O Holy Spirit, Enter In Come Down, O Love Divine	To God The Holy Spirit Let Us Pray Come, Holy Ghost, Our Souls Inspire Come, Holy Ghost, God, And Lord Lord God, The Holy Ghost

Weekly Record

Date						
Entrance Hymn						
Hymn Of The Day						
Anthem/ Special Music						
Sermon Title						
Lay Reader						
Attendance						

Holy Trinity Sunday

LESSON	CYCLE A	CYCLE B	CYCLE C
	Revised Common	**Revised Common**	**Revised Common**
First	Genesis 1:1—2:4a	Isaiah 6:1-8	Proverbs 8:1-4, 22-31
Second	2 Corinthians 13:11-13	Romans 8:12-17	Romans 5:1-5
Gospel	Matthew 28:16-20	John 3:1-17	John 16:12-15
	Episcopal	**Episcopal**	**Episcopal**
First	Genesis 1:1—2:3	Exodus 3:1-6	Isaiah 6:1-8
Second	2 Corinthians 13:(5-10) 11-14	Romans 8:12-17	Revelation 4:1-11
Gospel	Matthew 28:16-20	John 3:1-16	John 16:(5-11) 12-15
	Lutheran	**Lutheran**	**Lutheran**
First	Genesis 1:1—2:3	Deuteronomy 6:4-9	Proverbs 8:22-31
Second	2 Corinthians 13:11-14	Romans 8:14-17	Romans 5:1-5
Gospel	Matthew 28:16-20	John 3:1-17	John 16:12-15
	Roman Catholic	**Roman Catholic**	**Roman Catholic**
First	Exodus 34:4b-6, 8-9	Deuteronomy 4:32-34, 39-40	Proverbs 8:22-31
Second	2 Corinthians 13:11-13	Romans 8:14-17	Romans 5:1-5
Gospel	John 3:16-18	Matthew 28:16-20	John 16:12-15

Notes	Special Notes For A	Special Notes For B	Special Notes For C
Creed: Athanasian **Color:** White **Special Notation:** We believe in the God who led Israel and the God who reveals his loving and saving nature in Jesus, a confession that is made real only by the Holy Spirit.	The lessons point to the mystery of God and his unfathomable love for the life of the whole world. The commission of Matthew has been called "the key to the gospel." Might play tape of waves, wind and rain during the Genesis account of creation.	Series of 3 banners, connected in design or color could symbolize the Trinity. These could become one banner when placed together. Or 3-sided mobile banner could be created.	The intent of God seen in creation is renewed and fulfilled in the ministry and triumph of the Son and the sending of the Spirit. Though God is one, he has chosen to reveal himself in three persons, working through all three to lead us to the truth. Athanasian Creed could be read responsively with minister or congregation divided into two sections.

Music For Worship For Holy Trinity Sunday

NOTES	CYCLE A	CYCLE B	CYCLE C
	Creator Spirit, Heavenly Dove All Glory Be To God On High Lord, Keep Us Steadfast In Your Word Holy, Holy, Holy Glory, Be To God The Father Kyrie, God, Father In Heav'n Above Creator Spirit, By Whose Aid Thy Strong Word Alleluia, Sing To Jesus Spread, Oh Spread, Almighty Word	Father Most Holy I Bind Unto Myself Today All Glory Be To God On High Holy Spirit, Truth Divine O Trinity, O Blessed Light God The Father, Be Our Stay Eternal God, Before Your Throne We All Believe In One True God God, Whose Almighty Word Come, Thou Almighty King Holy God, We Praise Your Name	Creator Spirit, Heavenly Dove All Glory Be To God On High Come, Thou Almighty King Eternal God, Before Your Throne God The Father Be Our Stay God, Whose Almighty Word Holy Spirit, Truth Divine I Bind Unto Myself Today O Trinity, O Blessed Light We All Believe In One True God

Weekly Record

Date			
Entrance Hymn			
Hymn Of The Day			
Anthem/ Special Music			
Sermon Title			
Lay Reader			
Attendance			

Proper 4 — Pentecost 2 — OT 9

Readings

LESSON	CYCLE A	CYCLE B	CYCLE C
	Revised Common	**Revised Common**	**Revised Common**
First	Genesis 6:9-22; 7:24; 8:14-19	1 Samuel 3:1-10 (11-20)	1 Kings 18:20-21 (22-29) 30-39
Second	Romans 1:16-17; 3:22b-28 (29-31)	2 Corinthians 4:5-12	Galatians 1:1-12
Gospel	Matthew 7:21-29	Mark 2:23—3:6	Luke 7:1-10
	Episcopal	**Episcopal**	**Episcopal**
First	Deuteronomy 11:18-21, 26-28	Deuteronomy 5:6-21	1 Kings 8:22-23, 27-30, 41-43
Second	Romans 3:21-25a, 28	2 Corinthians 4:5-12	Galatians 1:1-10
Gospel	Matthew 7:21-27	Mark 2:23-28	Luke 7:1-10
	Lutheran	**Lutheran**	**Lutheran**
First	Deuteronomy 11:18-21, 26-28	Deuteronomy 5:12-15	1 Kings 8:(22-23, 27-30) 41-43
Second	Romans 3:21-25a, 27-28	2 Corinthians 4:5-12	Galatians 1:1-10
Gospel	Matthew 7:(15-20) 21-29	Mark 2:23-28	Luke 7:1-10
	Roman Catholic	**Roman Catholic**	**Roman Catholic**
First	Deuteronomy 11:18, 25-28, 32	Deuteronomy 5:12-15	1 Kings 8:22-23, 41-43
Second	Romans 3:21-25, 28	2 Corinthians 4:6-11	Galatians 1:1-2, 6-10
Gospel	Matthew 7:21-27	Mark 2:23—3:6	Luke 7:1-10

Notes	Special Notes For A	Special Notes For B	Special Notes For C
Creed: Apostles' **Color:** Green **Special Notation:** Jesus' eating and healing on the Sabbath	Here are God's demands upon those who would be among the faithful. Our speech and actions should be consistent with social responsibility and without any pretense of having special spiritual gifts.	Theme is observance of Sabbath. Explain difference between Sabbath (Saturday) and Lord's Day (Sunday)	We find faith in many unlikely places. God is neither Jew nor Greek and is not limited by language or geography or human intelligence. He does not belong to us. We belong to him.

Music For Worship For Proper 4 — Pentecost 2 — OT 9

NOTES	CYCLE A	CYCLE B	CYCLE C
	To God The Holy Spirit Let Us Pray Holy Spirit, Truth Divine Lord, Whose Love In Humble Service Lord Of All Nations, Grant Me Grace Maker Of The Earth And Heaven Oh, That The Lord Would Guide My Ways O Holy Spirit, Enter In Jesus, Still Lead On Amazing Grace, How Sweet The Sound Dear Christians, One And All If God Himself Be For Me In Thee Is Gladness	Holy Spirit, Truth Divine The First Day Of The Week O Day Of Rest And Gladness All Depends On Our Possessing From God Can Nothing Move Me O God, My Faithful God	To God The Holy Spirit Let Us Pray My Hope Is Built On Nothing Less Holy Spirit, Truth Divine

Weekly Record

Date						
Entrance Hymn						
Hymn Of The Day						
Anthem/ Special Music						
Sermon Title						
Lay Reader						
Attendance						

Proper 5 — Pentecost 3 — OT 10

Readings

LESSON	CYCLE A	CYCLE B	CYCLE C
	Revised Common	**Revised Common**	**Revised Common**
First	Genesis 12:1-9	2 Samuel 8:4-11 (12-12) 16-20, (11:14-15)	1 Kings 17:8-16 (17-24)
Second	Romans 4:13-25	2 Corinthians 4:13—5:1	Galatians 1:11-24
Gospel	Matthew 9:9-13, 18-26	Mark 3:20-35	Luke 7:11-17
	Episcopal	**Episcopal**	**Episcopal**
First	Hosea 6:3-6	Genesis 3:(1-7) 8-21	1 Kings 17:17-24
Second	Romans 4:18-25	2 Corinthians 4:13-18	Galatians 1:11-24
Gospel	Matthew 9:9-13	Mark 3:20-35	Luke 7:11-17
	Lutheran	**Lutheran**	**Lutheran**
First	Hosea 5:15—6:6	Genesis 3:9-15	1 Kings 17:17-24
Second	Romans 4:18-25	2 Corinthians 4:13-18	Galatians 1:11-24
Gospel	Matthew 9:9-13	Mark 3:20-35	Luke 7:11-17
	Roman Catholic	**Roman Catholic**	**Roman Catholic**
First	Hosea 6:3-6	Genesis 3:9-15	1 Kings 17:17-24
Second	Romans 4:18-25	2 Corinthians 4:13—5:1	Galatians 1:11-19
Gospel	Matthew 9:9-13	Mark 3:20-35	Luke 7:11-17
Notes	**Special Notes For A**	**Special Notes For B**	**Special Notes For C**

Notes

Creed: Apostles'
Color: Green
Special Notation: We must distinguish between good and evil and can do so only by looking at Jesus.

Special Notes For A

God came to serve and call those who are in need of being redeemed. People must acknowledge their need of God's saving grace and then consider carefully what that means for present-day disciples as they carry the ministry of Jesus to other sinners.

Special Notes For B

Adam and Eve were the original "blamers" with Adam blaming Eve and Eve blaming the serpent. This flaw is still a part of human nature, and we must learn to take responsibility for our actions, confess them and obtain forgiveness, so that we can love others in truth and be an acceptable listener and sharer.

Special Notes For C

Healing originates in compassion. What appears miraculous to us is another way to demonstrate God's remarkable love. When seen with eyes of faith, we are led to look beyond the healing to the Creator, and the response can only be fear, awe and a need to witness. Pray for healing and physical wholeness.

Music For Worship For Proper 5 — Pentecost 3 — OT 10

NOTES

CYCLE A

Oh, For A Thousand Tongues To Sing
When In The Hour Of Deepest Need
Dear Christians, One And All
To You, Omniscient Lord Of All
Today Your Mercy Calls Us
There's A Wilderness
The God Of Abraham Praise
By All Your Saints In Warfare
One There Is, Above All Others
"Come Follow Me," The Savior Spake

CYCLE B

Oh, For A Thousand Tongues To Sing
In Adam We Have All Been One
Praise The Savior, Now And Ever
O God, Our Help In Ages Past
On Our Way Rejoicing
My Heart Is Longing

CYCLE C

Jesus Sinners Will Receive
Oh, For A Thousand Tongues To Sing
Even As We Live Each Day
Oh, Sing, My Soul, Your Maker's Praise
From God Can Nothing Move Me

Weekly Record

Date			
Entrance Hymn			
Hymn Of The Day			
Anthem/ Special Music			
Sermon Title			
Lay Reader			
Attendance			

Proper 6 — Pentecost 4 — OT 11

Readings

LESSON	CYCLE A	CYCLE B	CYCLE C
	Revised Common	**Revised Common**	**Revised Common**
First	Genesis 18:1-15 (21:1-7)	1 Samuel 15:34—16:13	1 Kings 21:1-10 (11-14) 15-21a
Second	Romans 5:1-8	2 Corinthians 5:6-10, (11-13) 14-17	Galatians 2:15-21
Gospel	Matthew 9:35—10:8 (9-23)	Mark 4:26-34	Luke 7:36—8:3
	Episcopal	**Episcopal**	**Episcopal**
First	Exodus 19:2-8a	Ezekiel 31:1-6, 10-14	2 Samuel 11:26—12:10, 13-15
Second	Romans 5:6-11	2 Corinthians 5:1-10	Galatians 2:11-21
Gospel	Matthew 9:35—10:8	Mark 4:26-34	Luke 7:36-50
	Lutheran	**Lutheran**	**Lutheran**
First	Exodus 19:2-8a	Ezekiel 17:22-24	2 Samuel 11:26—12:10, 13-15
Second	Romans 5:6-11	2 Corinthians 5:1-10	Galatians 2:11-21
Gospel	Matthew 9:35—10:8	Mark 4:26-34	Luke 7:36-50
	Roman Catholic	**Roman Catholic**	**Roman Catholic**
First	Exodus 19:2-6a	Ezekiel 17:22-24	2 Samuel 12:7-10, 13
Second	Romans 5:6-11	2 Corinthians 5:6-10	Galatians 2:16, 19-21
Gospel	Matthew 9:36—10:8	Mark 4:26-34	Luke 7:36—8:3

Notes	Special Notes For A	Special Notes For B	Special Notes For C
Creed: Apostles' **Color:** Green **Special Notation:** God is in control. He has power over life and death, power to bring salvation to all kinds of people who will rest in the shade of his tree.	In order for the church to be truly apostolic, its people must be out in the world ministering to the needs of people in the name of God and through the love of God.	Parable of mustard seed. God works secretly in his own way. As Christians, we have 2 lives to live — one "in the body," and the second "home with the Lord." Our one goal is obedience.	God holds us accountable for our transgressions, particularly those against the poor. Sinners who respond in faith to God discover a wideness in his mercy, hearing "Your sins are forgiven."

NOTES	CYCLE A	CYCLE B	CYCLE C
	O God, O Lord Of Heaven And Earth Almighty God, Your Word Is Cast O Jesus, Joy Of Loving Hearts Jesus, Priceless Treasure A Mighty Fortress Is Our God God, My Lord, My Strength In Adam We Have All Been One Praise And Thanksgiving And Adoration Once He Came In Blessing	Almighty God, Your Word Is Cast We Know That Christ Is Raised Love Divine, All Loves Excelling Lord, Take My Hand And Lead Me Jesus, Savior, Pilot Me Eternal Father, Strong To Save I Am Trusting You, Lord Jesus	O God, O Lord Of Heaven And Earth Spread, Oh, Spread, Almighty Word Almighty God, Your Word Is Cast Baptized Into Your Name Most Holy In Christ There Is No East Or West "Take Up Your Cross," The Savior Said Let Us Ever Walk With Jesus

Weekly Record

Date			
Entrance Hymn			
Hymn Of The Day			
Anthem/ Special Music			
Sermon Title			
Lay Reader			
Attendance			

Readings

LESSON	CYCLE A	CYCLE B	CYCLE C
	Revised Common	**Revised Common**	**Revised Common**
First	Genesis 21:8-21	1 Samuel 17:(1a, 4-11, 19-23) 32-49	1 Kings 19:1-4 (5-7) 8-15a
Second	Romans 6:1b-11	2 Corinthians 6:1-13	Galatians 3:23-29
Gospel	Matthew 10:24-39	Mark 4:35-41	Luke 8:26-39
	Episcopal	**Episcopal**	**Episcopal**
First	Jeremiah 20:7-13	Job 38:1-11, 16-18	Zechariah 12:8-10, 13:1
Second	Romans 5:15b-19	2 Corinthians 5:14-21	Galatians 3:23-29
Gospel	Matthew 10:(16-23) 24-33	Mark 4:35-41 (5:1-20)	Luke 9:18-24
	Lutheran	**Lutheran**	**Lutheran**
First	Jeremiah 20:7-13	Job 38:1-11	Zechariah 12:7-10
Second	Romans 5:12-15	2 Corinthians 5:14-21	Galatians 3:23-29
Gospel	Matthew 10:24-33	Mark 4:35-41	Luke 9:18-24
	Roman Catholic	**Roman Catholic**	**Roman Catholic**
First	Jeremiah 20:10-13	Job 38:1, 8-11	Zechariah 12:10-11
Second	Romans 5:12-15	2 Corinthians 5:14-17	Galatians 3:26-29
Gospel	Matthew 10:26-33	Mark 4:35-41	Luke 9:18-24

Notes

Creed: Apostles'

Color: Green

Special Notation: The love of Christ has changed us. We look at other people with eyes of love and forgiveness because we are ambassadors for Christ.

Special Notes For A

Emphasis is on the call to a fearless posture regarding persecution. Jesus offers comfort to all who give a bold witness and suffer as a result of their faith. We might want to identify those of the faith who are currently being persecuted.

Special Notes For B

Everything we have, be it owned, rented, given or earned, came from the Lord. Someday it will all be broken, burned, lost, stolen or left behind when we die. Even members of our family, friends and the body we walk around in are lent to us.

Special Notes For C

Peter knew that Jesus was the fulfillment of the Old Testament promise. But he did not understand that it meant Christ was to suffer for the sake of the world. Those who would be disciples are invited to "put on Christ" and learn that "whoever would save his life will lose it and whoever loses his life for Christ's sake will save it." Pray for strength through suffering.

NOTES

CYCLE A	CYCLE B	CYCLE C
Lord Of Our Life Who Trusts In God, A Strong Abode Christ Is Made The Sure Foundation Awake, O Spirit, Of The Watchmen Your Kingdom come, O Father Praise The Lord, Rise Up Rejoicing All People That On Earth Do Dwell Before Jehovah's Awesome Throne O God Of Light Oh, Sing Jubilee To The Lord Open Now Thy Gates Of Beauty O Lord, We Praise You Chief Of Sinners Though I Be What Wondrous Love Is This Hark, The Voice Of Jesus Calling The Son Of God, Our Christ	Lord Of Our Life In Heaven Above Spirit Of God, Sent From Heaven Above Come, You Thankful People, Come Lord Our God, With Praise We Come	Lord Of Our Life Let Me Be Yours Forever Who Trusts In God, A Strong Abode Out Of The Depths I Cry To You Dear Christians, One And All Today Your Mercy Calls Us

Weekly Record

Date						
Entrance Hymn						
Hymn Of The Day						
Anthem/ Special Music						
Sermon Title						
Lay Reader						
Attendance						

Proper 8 — Pentecost 6 — OT 13

Readings

LESSON	CYCLE A	CYCLE B	CYCLE C
	Revised Common	**Revised Common**	**Revised Common**
First	Genesis 22:1-14	2 Samuel 1:1, 17-27	2 Kings 2:1-2, 6-14
Second	Romans 6:12-23	2 Corinthians 8:7-15	Galatians 5:1, 13-25
Gospel	Matthew 10:40-42	Mark 5:21-43	Luke 9:51-62
	Episcopal	**Episcopal**	**Episcopal**
First	Isaiah 2:10-17	Deuteronomy 15:7-11	1 Kings 19:15-16, 19-21
Second	Romans 6:3-11	2 Corinthians 8:1-9, 13-15	Galatians 5:1, 13-25
Gospel	Matthew 10:34-42	Mark 5:22-24; 35b-43	Luke 9:51-62
	Lutheran	**Lutheran**	**Lutheran**
First	Jeremiah 28:5-9	Lamentations 3:22-33	1 Kings 19:14-21
Second	Romans 6:1b-11	2 Corinthians 8:1-9, 13-14	Galatians 5:1, 13-25
Gospel	Matthew 10:34-42	Mark 5:21-24b, 35-43	Luke 9:51-62
	Roman Catholic	**Roman Catholic**	**Roman Catholic**
First	2 Kings 4:8-11, 14-16	Wisdom 1:13-15; 2:23-24	1 Kings 19:16b, 19-21
Second	Romans 6:3-4, 8-11	2 Corinthians 8:7, 9, 13-15	Galatians 5:1, 13-18
Gospel	Matthew 10:37-42	Mark 5:21-43	Luke 9:51-62

Notes	Special Notes For A	Special Notes For B	Special Notes For C
Creed: Apostles' Color: Green Special Notation: Because God's love has been so graciously revealed to us in Jesus, we are moved to share the blessings in meeting the needs of those who have so little.	The evangelist is broadening the audience to include all people who are disciples of Jesus. Discipleship is costly and valuable and may remain only at great sacrifice. This view challenges our gentle, serene fantasies about life as a part of the faithful.	Theme is hope and patience in the face of adversity.	The call to follow Jesus means he must come before all other relationships. We must abandon any other security and be entirely committed and totally dedicated to Christ and his mission. Pray for the mission of the church and for justice and peace.

Music For Worship For Proper 8 — Pentecost 6 — OT 13

NOTES

CYCLE A

Even As We Live Each Day
O God Of Mercy, God Of Light
Jesus, Thy Boundless Love To Me
O God, I Love Thee
Joyful, Joyful We Adore Thee
O God, Send Heralds
We Know That Christ Is Raised
All Who Believe And Are Baptized
Let Us Ever Walk With Jesus
"Take Up Your Cross," The Savior Said

CYCLE B

O God Of Mercy, God Of Light
If You But Trust In God To Guide You
I Trust, O Christ, In You Alone
Oh, Sing, My Soul, Your Maker's Praise
God, Whose Giving Knows No Ending
Lord Of All Good
O Christ, The Healer, We Have Come
Your Hand, O Lord In Days Of Old
How Sweet The Name Of Jesus Sounds

CYCLE C

Even As We Live Each Day
O God Of Mercy, God Of Light
O God, Send Heralds
When All Your Mercies, O My God
O Jesus, I Have Promised!
Forth In Thy Name O Lord, I Go
Spirit Of God, Descend Upon My Heart
In Thee Is Gladness
Lord, Thee I Love With All My Heart
Your Kingdom Come, O Father
"Come, Follow Me," The Savior Spake

Weekly Record

Date				
Entrance Hymn				
Hymn Of The Day				
Anthem/ Special Music				
Sermon Title				
Lay Reader				
Attendance				

Proper 9 — Pentecost 7 — OT 14

Readings

LESSON	CYCLE A	CYCLE B	CYCLE C
	Revised Common	**Revised Common**	**Revised Common**
First	Genesis 24:34-38, 42-49, 58-67	2 Samuel 5:1-5, 9-10	2 Kings 5:1-14
Second	Romans 7:15-25a	2 Corinthians 12:2-10	Galatians 6:(1-6) 7-16
Gospel	Matthew 11:16-19, 25-30	Mark 6:1-13	Luke 10:1-11, 16-20
	Episcopal	**Episcopal**	**Episcopal**
First	Zechariah 9:9-12	Ezekiel 2:1-7	Isaiah 66:1-16
Second	Romans 7:21—8:6	2 Corinthians 12:2-10	Galatians 6:(1-10) 14-18
Gospel	Matthew 11:25-30	Mark 6:1-6	Luke 10:1-12, 16-20
	Lutheran	**Lutheran**	**Lutheran**
First	Zechariah 9:9-12	Ezekiel 2:1-5	Isaiah 66:10-14
Second	Romans 7:15-25a	2 Corinthians 12:7-10	Galatians 6:1-10, 14-16
Gospel	Matthew 11:25-30	Mark 6:1-6	Luke 10:1-12, 16 (17-20)
	Roman Catholic	**Roman Catholic**	**Roman Catholic**
First	Zechariah 9:9-10	Ezekiel 2:2-5	Isaiah 66:10-14
Second	Romans 8:9, 11-13	2 Corinthians 12:7-10	Galatians 6:14-18
Gospel	Matthew 11:25-30	Mark 6:1-6	Luke 10:1-12, 17-20

Notes

Notes	Special Notes For A	Special Notes For B	Special Notes For C
Creed: Apostles' Color: Green Special Notation: Sometimes we struggle with ailments despite our prayers. We should try to see the strong side of weakness — the power of God using weak vessels like ourselves.	Today's lessons speak of how the humble and poor come to know the depth of God's being. In order to follow the pattern of the Master, we must witness to the truth by humble testimony and suffering for the truth's sake, not in an authoritarian manner.	God has been giving second chances all through history. How many times has he sent a prophet to the House of Israel? Even today the world still rebels, but his love remains steadfast, and we are called upon to be voices for Christ before it is too late. Suffering separates us from the world for a time, but brings us closer to God.	God is the giver of peace. Church people are the sent ones bearing the message of the gospel of the nearness of the kingdom of God. We are like lambs among wolves, but are assured of his presence and support. We live with a vision of a future kingdom where our hearts will rejoice and all will be well.

Music For Worship For Proper 9 — Pentecost 7 — OT 14

NOTES	CYCLE A	CYCLE B	CYCLE C
	A Christ, Our Light, O Radiance True God Moves In A Mysterious Way Jesus Shall Reign Rejoice, O Pilgrim Throng! Before You, Lord, We Bow All Creatures Of Our God And King Awake, My Soul, And With The Sun May We Your Precepts, Lord, Fulfill Come, Gracing Spirit, Heavenly Dove Oh, That The Lord Would Guide My Ways I Heard The Voice Of Jesus Say Forth In Thy Name, O Lord, I Go	God Moves In A Mysterious Way O God Of Light God Has Spoken By His Prophets Jesus, Still Lead On	O Christ, Our Light, O Radiance True Peace, To Soothe Our Bittersweet Woes God Moves In A Mysterious Way I Love To Tell The Story

Weekly Record

Date			
Entrance Hymn			
Hymn Of The Day			
Anthem/ Special Music			
Sermon Title			
Lay Reader			
Attendance			

Readings

LESSON		CYCLE A	CYCLE B	CYCLE C

CYCLE A

Revised Common
First — Genesis 25:19-34
Second — Romans 8:1-11
Gospel — Matthew 13:1-9, 18-23

Episcopal
First — Isaiah 55:10-11
Second — Romans 8:18-23
Gospel — Matthew 13:1-9, 18-23

Lutheran
First — Isaiah 55:10-11
Second — Romans 8:18-25
Gospel — Matthew 13:1-9 (18-23)

Roman Catholic
First — Isaiah 55:10-11
Second — Romans 8:18-23
Gospel — Matthew 13:1-23

CYCLE B

Revised Common
First — 2 Samuel 6:1-5, 12b-19
Second — Ephesians 1:3-14
Gospel — Mark 6:14-29

Episcopal
First — Amos 7:7-15
Second — Ephesians 1:1-14
Gospel — Mark 6:7-13

Lutheran
First — Amos 7:10-15
Second — Ephesians 1:3-14
Gospel — Mark 6:7-13

Roman Catholic
First — Amos 7:12-15
Second — Ephesians 1:3-14
Gospel — Mark 6:7-13

CYCLE C

Revised Common
First — Amos 7:7-17
Second — Colossians 1:1-14
Gospel — Luke 10:25-37

Episcopal
First — Deuteronomy 30:9-14
Second — Colossians 1:1-14
Gospel — Luke 10:25-37

Lutheran
First — Deuteronomy 30:9-14
Second — Colossians 1:1-14
Gospel — Luke 10:25-37

Roman Catholic
First — Deuteronomy 30:10-14
Second — Colossians 1:15-20
Gospel — Luke 10:25-37

Notes

Creed: Apostles'
Color: Green
Special Notation: You can only be a prophet if God makes you one. God's people are ordinary except in that they are his.

Special Notes For A

The parable of the sower gives hope and encouragement to disciples who are discouraged and frustrated. Regardless of what seems to impede the progress and development of the kingdom, God guarantees the harvest. The ministry of the faithful is supported and lifted in the midst of the troubles of the moment.

Special Notes For B

Important words about Jesus: love, blood, forgiveness, grace, will, glory, truth, gospel, peace. Important words for us: faith, praise.

Special Notes For C

We should not ask, "Who is my neighbor?" but rather, "To whom am I acting as a neighbor?" We must move from abstractions to specific acts of love and charity. Pray for poor and neglected and a breaking down of barriers to brotherhood.

NOTES

CYCLE A	CYCLE B	CYCLE C
Forth In Thy Name, O Lord, I Go The Son Of God, Our Christ O God Of Mercy, God Of Light To God, The Holy Spirit Let Us Pray Eternal Spirit Of The Living Christ Your Word, O Lord, Is Gentle Dew Sent Forth By God's Blessing When Seed Falls On Good Soil Open Now Thy Gates Of Beauty On What Has Now Been Sown	The Son Of God, Our Christ The Lord Will Come And Not Be Slow Dear Christians, One And All O God, O Lord Of Heaven And Earth From God Can Nothing Move Me God Moves In A Mysterious Way O God Of God, O Light Of Light	Forth In Thy Name, O Lord, I Go Almighty God, Your Word Is Cast The Song Of God, Our Christ How Blest Are They Who Hear God's Word O God Of Love, O King Of Peace Hope Of The World Lead On, O King Eternal For The Fruit Of All Creation

Weekly Record

Date			
Entrance Hymn			
Hymn Of The Day			
Anthem/ Special Music			
Sermon Title			
Lay Reader			
Attendance			

Proper 11 — Pentecost 9 — OT 16

Readings

LESSON	CYCLE A	CYCLE B	CYCLE C
	Revised Common	**Revised Common**	**Revised Common**
First	Genesis 28:10-19a	2 Samuel 7:1-14a	Amos 8:1-12
Second	Romans 8:12-25	Ephesians 2:11-22	Colossians 1:15-28
Gospel	Matthew 13:24-30, 36-43	Mark 6:30-44, 53-56	Luke 10:38-42
	Episcopal	**Episcopal**	**Episcopal**
First	Wisdom 12:13, 16-19	Isaiah 57:14b-21	Genesis 18:1-10a (10b-14)
Second	Romans 8:18-25	Ephesians 2:11-22	Colossians 1:21-29
Gospel	Matthew 13:24-30, 36-43	Mark 6:30-44	Luke 10:38-42
	Lutheran	**Lutheran**	**Lutheran**
First	Isaiah 44:6-8	Jeremiah 23:1-6	Genesis 18:1-10a (10b-14)
Second	Romans 8:26-27	Ephesians 2:13-22	Colossians 1:21-28
Gospel	Matthew 13:24-30 (36-43)	Mark 6:30-34	Luke 10:38-42
	Roman Catholic	**Roman Catholic**	**Roman Catholic**
First	Wisdom 12:13, 16-19	Jeremiah 23:1-6	Genesis 18:1-10a
Second	Romans 8:26-27	Ephesians 2:13-18	Colossians 1:24-28
Gospel	Matthew 13:24-30, 36-43	Mark 6:30-34	Luke 10:38-42

Notes	Special Notes For A	Special Notes For B	Special Notes For C
Creed: Apostles' **Color:** Green **Special Notation:** Christ is the true shepherd, the people's shepherd, who labors tirelessly to lead and teach us all.	In the parable of the weeds, a note of assurance is sounded regarding the harvest, but there is also a warning against impatience and judgment. The fact and presence of evil in ourselves and in our world cannot be allowed to divert us from the work of the kingdom.	The Lord pronounces judgment on false prophets and promises that he will raise up a branch of David whose name shall be "the Lord our righteousness." Through his great love, Christ has abolished the enmity between us and made us members of God's household.	Luke tells us that the Christian life is both concrete acts of love and listening to the Lord. It is a journey outward and a journey inward. Unless directed by the Word of God, our good deeds run the danger of being merely busy work.

Music For Worship For Proper 11 — Pentecost 9 — OT 16

NOTES

CYCLE A

O Holy Spirit, Enter In
O God Of Light
Lord, Thee I Love With All My Heart
Holy Spirit, Truth Divine
Eternal God, Before Your Throne
Come, Oh, Come, O Quickening Spirit
Dear Lord And Father Of Mankind
Eternal Spirit Of That Living Christ
How Blest Are They Who Hear God's Word
There's A Wideness In God's Mercy
The Lord Will Come And Not Be Slow
Come You Thankful People, Come
The God Of Abraham Praise

CYCLE B

O God Of Light
Praise The Lord, Rise Up Rejoicing
The Lord's My Shepherd
The King Of Love My Shepherd Is
Who Trusts In God, A Strong Abode
Lord, Receive This Company
Through The Night Of Doubt And Sorrow
Christ Is Made The Sure Foundation
The Church's One Foundation
Whatever God Ordains Is Right
Lord, Who The Night You Were Betrayed

CYCLE C

O Holy Spirit, Enter In
On What Has Now Been Sown
O God Of Light
Have No Fear, Little Flock

Weekly Record

Date			
Entrance Hymn			
Hymn Of The Day			
Anthem/ Special Music			
Sermon Title			
Lay Reader			
Attendance			

Proper 12 — Pentecost 10 — OT 17

Readings

LESSON	CYCLE A	CYCLE B	CYCLE C
	Revised Common	**Revised Common**	**Revised Common**
First	Genesis 29:15-28	2 Samuel 11:1-15	Hosea 1:2-10
Second	Romans 8:26-39	Ephesians 3:14-21	Colossians 2:6-15 (16-19)
Gospel	Matthew 13:31-33, 44-52	John 6:1-21	Luke 11:1-13
	Episcopal	**Episcopal**	**Episcopal**
First	1 Kings 3:5-12	2 Kings 2:1-15	Genesis 18:20-33
Second	Romans 8:26-34	Ephesians 4:1-7, 11-16	Colossians 2:6-15
Gospel	Matthew 13:31-33, 44-49a	Mark 6:45-52	Luke 11:1-13
	Lutheran	**Lutheran**	**Lutheran**
First	1 Kings 3:5-12	Exodus 24:3-11	Genesis 18:20-32
Second	Romans 8:28-30	Ephesians 4:1-7, 11-16	Colossians 2:6-15
Gospel	Matthew 13:44-52	John 6:1-15	Luke 11:1-13
	Roman Catholic	**Roman Catholic**	**Roman Catholic**
First	1 Kings 3:5, 7-12	2 Kings 4:42-44	Genesis 18:20-32
Second	Romans 8:28-30	Ephesians 4:1-6	Colossians 2:12-14
Gospel	Matthew 13:44-52	John 6:1-15	Luke 11:1-13

Notes	Special Notes For A	Special Notes For B	Special Notes For C
Cred: Apostles' **Color:** Green **Special Notation:** Miraculous feeding of 5,000 reminds us of feasting of people at Mount Sinai when God made his covenant with them.	The two parables of the hidden treasure and pearl of great value speak about the ultimate worth and importance of the kingdom. Just as a person would expend great amounts of energy and resources to find and acquire worldly treasure, so the disciple of Jesus is called upon to hold the kingdom in such high regard that no price is too high to attain it.	Paul asks for unity among believers and the living of a life worthy of the calling we have received. Closeness comes with love. Love is patient, humble and gentle. The gospel reminds us that anything is possible with Jesus. Sunday school children might be asked their reaction if they invited some people to a picnic and 5,000 showed up!	God knows our needs better than we do and he hears and answers every prayer. Jesus gave his disciples a special prayer and invited us to pray expectantly and persistently.

Music For Worship For Proper 12 — Pentecost 10 — OT 17

NOTES	CYCLE A	CYCLE B	CYCLE C
	From God Can Nothing Move Me Jesus, Priceless Treasure Lord, Teach Us Now To Pray Aright	From God Can Nothing Move Me Before You, Lord, We Bow All Creatures Of Our God And King Praise And Thanksgiving Be To God Through The Night Of Doubt And Sorrow The Church's One Foundation Blest Be The Tie That Binds Come Down, Love Divine Onward Christian Soldiers Break Now The Bread Of Life	**Handel Hymns** Joy To The World Thine Is The Glory **Bach Arrangements** Let The Whole Creation Cry (Entrance) Come With Us, O Blessed Jesus (Communion) From God Can Nothing Move Me O God, O Lord Of Heaven And Earth Jesus, Priceless Treasure

Weekly Record

Date			
Entrance Hymn			
Hymn Of The Day			
Anthem/ Special Music			
Sermon Title			
Lay Reader			
Attendance			

Proper 13 — Pentecost 11 — OT 18

Readings

LESSON	CYCLE A	CYCLE B	CYCLE C
	Revised Common	**Revised Common**	**Revised Common**
First	Genesis 32:22-31	2 Samuel 11:26—12:13a	Hosea 11:1-11
Second	Romans 9:1-5	Ephesians 4:1-16	Colossians 3:1-11
Gospel	Matthew 14:13-21	John 6:24-35	Luke 12:13-21
	Episcopal	**Episcopal**	**Episcopal**
First	Nehemiah 9:16-20	Exodus 16:2-4, 9-15	Ecclesiastes 1:12-14; 2:(1-7, 11) 18-23
Second	Romans 8:35-39	Ephesians 4:17-25	Colossians 3:(5-11) 12-17
Gospel	Matthew 14:13-21	John 6:24-35	Luke 12:13-21
	Lutheran	**Lutheran**	**Lutheran**
First	Isaiah 55:1-5	Exodus 16:2-15	Ecclesiastes 1:2; 2:18-26
Second	Romans 8:35-39	Ephesians 4:17-24	Colossians 3:1-11
Gospel	Matthew 14:13-21	John 6:24-35	Luke 12:13-21
	Roman Catholic	**Roman Catholic**	**Roman Catholic**
First	Isaiah 55:1-3	Exodus 16:2-4, 12-15	Ecclesiastes 1:2; 2:21-23
Second	Romans 8:35, 37-39	Ephesians 4:17, 20-24	Colossians 3:1-5, 9-11
Gospel	Matthew 14:13-21	John 6:24-35	Luke 12:13-21

Notes

Creed: Apostles'
Color: Green
Special Notation: Sharp contrast between ways of the world and ways of Christ. This difference between old nature and new nature shows up in the way we live.

Special Notes For A

Attention is given to food and drink in the lives of the faithful. We are drawn to communion and the way it nourishes us. The prayer of the day speaks of Jesus as the true bread which gives life to the world. Visuals could be loaves and fish.

Special Notes For B

The Lord sends meat and bread to the hungry children of Israel, following the Exodus. The Lord again sends manna from heaven to the Jews in the person of Jesus who is the Bread of Life. Words used to describe unbelievers: darkness, ignorance, insensitive, impure, lustful, futile, deceitful, vain, greedy, corrupt. Words for those who have put on Christ: children of light, truth, renewal, new self, righteous, holy.

Special Notes For C

The first lesson could be introduced in this manner: "The writer of Ecclesiastes is a skeptic who doubts nearly everything that the wise men of his day taught. He sees no proof that the wise man in this world is happier or more prosperous than one who is either a fool or wicked."

NOTES

CYCLE A	CYCLE B	CYCLE C
Jesus, Priceless Treasure O Bread Of Life From Heaven Son Of God, Eternal Savior	O Bread Of Life From Heaven Glories Of Your Name Are Spoken How Sweet The Name Of Jesus Sounds Love Divine, All Loves Excelling Breathe On Me, Breath Of God O God, My Faithful God O Living Bread From Heaven Here, O My Lord, I See Thee Soul, Adorn Yourself With Gladness Guide Me Ever, Great Redeemer O Lord, Send Forth Your Spirit	Jesus, Priceless Treasure Praise And Thanksgiving O Bread Of Life From Heaven May We Your Precepts, Lord, Fulfill In Christ There Is No East Or West Eternal Ruler Of The Ceaseless Round Oh, That The Lord Would Guide My Ways O God, My Faithful God Renew Me, O Eternal Light God Of Grace And God Of Glory Lord, Save Your World

Weekly Record

Date					
Entrance Hymn					
Hymn Of The Day					
Anthem/ Special Music					
Sermon Title					
Lay Reader					
Attendance					

Readings

LESSON	CYCLE A	CYCLE B	CYCLE C
	Revised Common	**Revised Common**	**Revised Common**
First	Genesis 37:1-4, 12-28	2 Samuel 18:5-9, 15, 31-33	Isaiah 1:1; 10-20
Second	Romans 10:5-15	Ephesians 4:25—5:2	Hebrews 11:1-3, 8-16
Gospel	Matthew 14:22-33	John 6:35, 41-51	Luke 12:32-40
	Episcopal	**Episcopal**	**Episcopal**
First	Jonah 2:1-9	Deuteronomy 8:1-10	Genesis 15:1-6
Second	Romans 9:1-5	Ephesians 4:(25-29) 30—5:2	Hebrews 11:1-3 (4-7) 8-16
Gospel	Matthew 14:22-33	John 6:41-51	Luke 12:32-40
	Lutheran	**Lutheran**	**Lutheran**
First	1 Kings 19:9-18	1 Kings 19:4-8	Genesis 15:1-6
Second	Romans 9:1-5	Ephesians 4:30—5:2	Hebrews 11:1-3, 8-16
Gospel	Matthew 14:22-33	John 6:41-51	Luke 12:32-40
	Roman Catholic	**Roman Catholic**	**Roman Catholic**
First	1 Kings 19:9, 11-13	1 Kings 19:4-8	Wisdom 18:6-9
Second	Romans 9:1-5	Ephesians 4:30—5:2	Hebrews 11:1-2, 8-19
Gospel	Matthew 14:22-33	John 6:41-51	Luke 12:32-48

Notes	Special Notes For A	Special Notes For B	Special Notes For C
Creed: Apostles' **Color:** Green **Special Notation:** We should be imitators of God in love, forgiveness, kindness and tenderheartedness.	The account of Jesus and Peter walking on the water calls attention to life's storms, our periods of little faith and encourages trust in Christ who is always present.	The theme of this week is Jesus' response to his critics, and his reiteration of the Bread of Life theme.	We are beloved children of a wealthy Father, who can live with the assurance of one who will soon inherit his kingdom. We should not waste time and energy gathering the kind of treasure that will rust and decay. Also, not knowing when the inheritance will take effect, we are urged to live in anticipation of his imminent return.

NOTES

CYCLE A

If God Himself Be For Me
Guide Me Ever Great Redeemer
Rise, My Soul, To Watch And Pray
Evening And Morning
Dear Lord And Father Of Mankind
The Lord Will Come And Not Be Slow
Lord, Take My Hand And Lead Me
Jesus, Savior, Pilot Me
Lord Of Our Life
Jesus, Priceless Treasure
From God Can Nothing Move Me

CYCLE B

Guide Me Ever, Great Redeemer
Forgive Our Sins As We Forgive
Joyful, Joyful, We Adore Thee
O Living Bread From Heaven
We Who Once Were Dead
O Bread Of Life From Heaven
Soul, Adorn Yourself With Gladness
O Jesus, Joy Of Loving Hearts
Draw Near And Take The Body Of The Lord

CYCLE C

If God Himself Be For Me
Eternal Father, Strong To Save
Guide Me, Ever, Great Redeemer
Have No Fear, Little Flock

Weekly Record

Date		
Entrance Hymn		
Hymn Of The Day		
Anthem/ Special Music		
Sermon Title		
Lay Reader		
Attendance		

Proper 15 — Pentecost 13 — OT 20

Readings

LESSON		CYCLE A	CYCLE B	CYCLE C
		Revised Common	**Revised Common**	**Revised Common**
First		Genesis 45:1-15	1 Kings 2:10-12; 3:3-14	Isaiah 5:1-7
Second		Romans 11:1-2a, 29-32	Ephesians 5:15-20	Hebrews 11:29—12:2
Gospel		Matthew 15:(10-20) 21-28	John 6:51-58	Luke 12:49-56
		Episcopal	**Episcopal**	**Episcopal**
First		Isaiah 56:1 (2-5) 6-7	Proverbs 9:1-6	Jeremiah 23:23-29
Second		Romans 11:13-15, 29-32	Ephesians 5:15-20	Hebrews 12:1-7 (8-10) 11-14
Gospel		Matthew 15:21-28	John 6:53-59	Luke 12:49-56
		Lutheran	**Lutheran**	**Lutheran**
First		Isaiah 56:1, 6-8	Proverbs 9:1-6	Jeremiah 23:23-29
Second		Romans 11:13-15, 29-32	Ephesians 5:15-20	Hebrews 12:1-13
Gospel		Matthew 15:21-28	John 6:51-58	Luke 12:49-53
		Roman Catholic	**Roman Catholic**	**Roman Catholic**
First		Isaiah 56:1, 6-7	Proverbs 9:1-6	Jeremiah 38:4-5
Second		Romans 11:13-15, 29-32	Ephesians 5:15-20	Hebrews 12:1-14
Gospel		Matthew 15:21-28	John 6:51-58	Luke 12:49-53

Notes

Creed: Apostles'

Color: Green

Special Notation: The Eucharist opens a close relationship to Christ, a communion that brings Christ's life into us. A Christian walk brings glory to God.

Special Notes For A

These lessons consider universalism — the gospel for all people. There is concern for God's faithfulness to Israel and the miracle of the faith of the gentiles. The deep belief of the Canaanite woman focuses on our discipleship and the critical factor of faith.

Special Notes For B

Theme is invitation to a banquet prepared by Wisdom. In the eating and drinking there comes life and insight.

Special Notes For C

The cross, which Jesus calls his baptism, is a symbol of his radical obedience to the will of God. Disciples are also called to that obedience, even if it leads to death. We are forced to choose between those things that are important and that which is ultimate. It may even be between that which is good and that which is excellent.

Music For Worship For Proper 15 — Pentecost 13 — OT 20

NOTES	CYCLE A	CYCLE B	CYCLE C
	How Blest Are They Who Hear God's Word Lord, Keep Us Steadfast In Your Word A Multitude Come From East And West In Christ There Is No East And West May God Bestow On Us This Grace To You, Omniscient Lord Of All Rise, Shine, You People Lord, Whose Love In Humble Service Father, We Praise You	How Blest Are They Who Hear God's Word Take My Life That I May Be Now Thank We All Our God When Morning Gilds The Skies When In Our Music God is Glorified Let All Things Now Living O Living Bread From Heaven We Who Once Were Dead O Bread Of Life From Heaven Soul, Adorn Yourself With Gladness O Jesus, Joy Of Loving Hearts	When In The Hour Of Deepest Need How Blest Are They Who Hear God's Word The Lord Will Come And Not Be Slow God, The Father Be Our Stay If You But Trust In God To Guide You Fight The Good Fight Evening And Morning God, My Lord, My Strength Thee Will I Love, My Strength How Firm A Foundation

Weekly Record

Date					
Entrance Hymn					
Hymn Of The Day					
Anthem/ Special Music					
Sermon Title					
Lay Reader					
Attendance					

Proper 16 — Pentecost 14 — OT 21

Readings

LESSON		CYCLE A	CYCLE B	CYCLE C
		Revised Common	**Revised Common**	**Revised Common**
First		Exodus 1:8—2:10	1 Kings 8:(1, 6, 10-11) 22-30, 41-43	Jeremiah 1:4-10
Second		Romans 12:1-8	Ephesians 6:10-20	Hebrews 12:18-29
Gospel		Matthew 16:13-20	John 6:56-69	Luke 13:10-17
		Episcopal	**Episcopal**	**Episcopal**
First		Isaiah 51:1-6	Joshua 24:1-2a, 14-25	Isaiah 28:14-22
Second		Romans 11:33-36	Ephesians 5:21-33	Hebrews 12:18-19, 22-29
Gospel		Matthew 16:13-20	John 6:60-69	Luke 13:22-30
		Lutheran	**Lutheran**	**Lutheran**
First		Exodus 6:2-8	Joshua 24:1-2a, 14-18	Isaiah 66:18-23
Second		Romans 11:33-36	Ephesians 5:21-31	Hebrews 12:18-24
Gospel		Matthew 16:13-20	John 6:60-69	Luke 13:22-30
		Roman Catholic	**Roman Catholic**	**Roman Catholic**
First		Isaiah 22:15, 19-23	Joshua 24:1-2, 15-18	Isaiah 66:18-21
Second		Romans 11:33-36	Ephesians 5:21-32	Hebrews 12:5-7, 11-13
Gospel		Matthew 16:13-20	John 6:60-69	Luke 13:22-30

Notes

Creed: Apostles'

Color: Green

Special Notation: We must always make a decision — the world or Christ. Marriage and home matters and family are explained from perspective of Christ's relationship to the church.

Special Notes For A

Here is strong affirmation of the faith of the disciples and the early church. The Lord replies that in naming and believing, the church will be built and will take on his character. As it gathers, it will bear his gifts to the world. That which marks the Christ will also, in some way, mark the life and quality of the people of God.

Special Notes For B

Emphasize "Lord to whom shall we go. You have the words of eternal life." This Sunday or next week is a good time to introduce Sunday school teachers and pray for them.

Special Notes For C

The kingdom is not a place but a process to achieve a person's salvation through Jesus Christ. The believer doesn't travel to a destination and then relax, but must live the striving to be part of this redeeming activity of God. Those who let their love grow cold and their work in the gospel slack off may lose God's gift of life entirely.

Music For Worship For Proper 16 — Pentecost 14 — OT 21

NOTES

CYCLE A	CYCLE B	CYCLE C
O Christ, Our Light, O Radiance True Hope Of The World A Multitude Come From East And West We Worship You, O God Of Might Jesus Shall Reign Holy God, We Praise Your Name Thee We Adore, Eternal Lord! The God Of Abraham Praise Blessing And Honor Immortal, Invisible, God Only Wise By All Your Saints In Warfare	Hope Of The World Our Father, By Whose Name Oh, Blest The House For The Beauty Of The Earth You Are The Way Let Me Be Your Forever O Jesus, I Have Promised	O Christ, Our Light, O Radiance True Built On A Rock Hope Of The World In Christ There Is No East Or West From All That Dwell Below The Skies

Weekly Record

Date					
Entrance Hymn					
Hymn Of The Day					
Anthem/ Special Music					
Sermon Title					
Lay Reader					
Attendance					

Proper 17 — Pentecost 15 — OT 22

Readings

LESSON	CYCLE A	CYCLE B	CYCLE C
	Revised Common	**Revised Common**	**Revised Common**
First	Exodus 3:1-5	Song Of Solomon 2:8-13	Jeremiah 2:4-13
Second	Romans 12:9-21	James 1:17-27	Hebrews 13:1-8, 15-16
Gospel	Matthew 16:21-28	Mark 7:1-8, 14-15, 21-23	Luke 14:1, 7-14
	Episcopal	**Episcopal**	**Episcopal**
First	Jeremiah 15:15-21	Deuteronomy 4:1-9	Ecclesiastes 10:(7-11), 12-18
Second	Romans 12:1-8	Ephesians 6:10-20	Hebrews 13:1-8
Gospel	Matthew 16:21-27	Mark 7:1-8, 14-15, 21-23	Luke 14:1, 7-14
	Lutheran	**Lutheran**	**Lutheran**
First	Jeremiah 15:15-21	Deuteronomy 4:1-2, 6-8	Proverbs 25:6-7
Second	Romans 12:1-8	Ephesians 6:10-20	Hebrews 13:1-8
Gospel	Matthew 16:21-26	Mark 7:1-8, 14-15, 21-23	Luke 14:1, 7-14
	Roman Catholic	**Roman Catholic**	**Roman Catholic**
First	Jeremiah 20:7-9	Deuteronomy 4:1-2, 6-8	Sirach 3:17-18, 20, 28-29
Second	Romans 12:1-2	James 1:17-18, 21-22, 27	Hebrews 12:18-19, 22-24a
Gospel	Matthew 16:21-27	Mark 7:1-8, 14-15, 21-23	Luke 14:1, 7-14

Notes	Special Notes For A	Special Notes For B	Special Notes For C
Creed: Apostles' **Color:** Green **Special Notation:** God's people are freed from striving to justify themselves.	This Sunday has two themes: Jesus' rebuke to Peter, and saving and losing life.	Christians' armor is truth and righteousness. It includes the gospel of peace and the shield of faith; wearing the helmet of salvation and carrying the sword of the Spirit, in prayer and supplication.	Is this a two-part lesson on how to obtain rewards when you go to or give a banquet; or is it a description of how things are at table in the kingdom of God?

NOTES

CYCLE A

Son Of God, Eternal Savior
To You, Omniscient Lord Of All
O God Of Earth And Altar
Maker Of The Earth And Heaven
God's Word Is Our Great Heritage
Where Charity And Love Prevail
Hark, The Voice Of Jesus Calling
"Take Up Your Cross," The Savior Said
"O Come, Follow Me," The Savior Spake
Praise And Thanks And Adoration
I Love Your Kingdom, Lord

CYCLE B

Son Of God, Eternal Savior
You Are The Way
Oh, That The Lord Would Guide My Ways
A Mighty Fortress Is Our God
Let The Whole Creation Cry
God The Father, Be Our Stay
We Sing The Praise Of Him Who Died
Do Not Despair, O Little Flock
Eternal Ruler Of The Ceaseless Round
Stand Up, Stand Up For Jesus
With The Lord Begin Your Task
Fight The Good Fight

CYCLE C

Son Of God, Eternal Savior
If God Himself Be For Me
To You, Omniscient Lord Of All
We Give Thee But Thine Own
Lord Of All Nations, Grant Me Grace
Where Cross The Crowded Ways Of Life
Lord, Whose Love In Humble Service

Weekly Record

Date					
Entrance Hymn					
Hymn Of The Day					
Anthem/ Special Music					
Sermon Title					
Lay Reader					
Attendance					

Readings

LESSON	CYCLE A	CYCLE B	CYCLE C
	Revised Common	**Revised Common**	**Revised Common**
First	Exodus 12:1-14	Proverbs 22:1-2, 8-9, 22-23	Jeremiah 18:1-11
Second	Romans 13:8-14	James 2:1-10 (11-13) 14-17	Philemon 1-21
Gospel	Matthew 18:15-20	Mark 7:24-37	Luke 14:25-33
	Episcopal	**Episcopal**	**Episcopal**
First	Ezekiel 33:(1-6) 7-11	Isaiah 35:4-7a	Deuteronomy 30:15-20
Second	Romans 12:9-21	James 1:17-27	Philemon 1-20
Gospel	Matthew 18:15-20	Mark 7:31-37	Luke 14:25-33
	Lutheran	**Lutheran**	**Lutheran**
First	Ezekiel 33:7-9	Isaiah 35:4-7a	Proverbs 9:8-12
Second	Romans 13:1-10	James 1:17-22 (23-25) 26-27	Philemon 1 (2-9) 10-21
Gospel	Matthew 18:15-20	Mark 7:31-37	Luke 14:25-33
	Roman Catholic	**Roman Catholic**	**Roman Catholic**
First	Ezekiel 33:7-9	Isaiah 35:4-7a	Wisdom 9:13-18
Second	Romans 13:8-10	James 2:1-5	Philemon 9b-10, 12-17
Gospel	Matthew 18:15-20	Mark 7:31-37	Luke 14:25-33

Notes	Special Notes For A	Special Notes For B	Special Notes For C
Creed: Apostles' **Color:** Green **Special Notation:** The disciples and those present when Jesus' power was seen in healing of deaf man burst forth in praise.	It is the work of Christ and the church to free all to be God's people and restore life to the world. What are those things that bind us and prevent our commitment? Self-interest drives us, but we are called to care for others.	Slides of various helping agencies, of people helping people, could be projected while Psalm 146 is read.	We say love is blind. Jesus seems to say he wants no blind followers. He wants us to clearly see the cost, and the cost is all that we have.

NOTES	CYCLE A	CYCLE B	CYCLE C
	Praise The Almighty O Son Of God, In Galilee Take My Life, That I May Be Awake, O Spirit Of The Watchmen O God Of Earth And Altar God Of Our Fathers Built On A Rock And Have The Bright Immensities	O Son Of God, In Galilee Look From Your Sphere Of Endless Day We Give Thee But Thine Own God, My Faithful God O Christ, Our Light, O Radiance True Son Of God, Eternal Savior	Praise The Almighty Lord Of All Nations, Grant Me Grace O Son Of God, In Galilee "Take Up Your Cross," The Savior Said Let Us Ever Walk With Jesus God, My Lord, My Strength

Weekly Record

Date			
Entrance Hymn			
Hymn Of The Day			
Anthem/ Special Music			
Sermon Title			
Lay Reader			
Attendance			

Proper 19 — Pentecost 17 — OT 24

Readings

LESSON	CYCLE A	CYCLE B	CYCLE C
	Revised Common	**Revised Common**	**Revised Common**
First	Exodus 14:19-31	Proverbs 1:20-33	Jeremiah 4:11-12, 22-28
Second	Romans 14:1-12	James 3:1-12	1 Timothy 1:12-17
Gospel	Matthew 18:21-35	Mark 8:27-38	Luke 15:1-10
	Episcopal	**Episcopal**	**Episcopal**
First	Ecclesiasticus 27:30—28:7	Isaiah 50:4-9	Exodus 32:1, 7-14
Second	Romans 14:5-12	James 2:1-5, 8-10, 14-18	1 Timothy 1:12-27
Gospel	Matthew 18:21-35	Mark 8:27-38	Luke 15:1-10
	Lutheran	**Lutheran**	**Lutheran**
First	Genesis 50:15-21	Isaiah 50:4-10	Exodus 32:7-14
Second	Romans 14:5-9	James 2:1-5, 8-10, 14-18	1 Timothy 1:12-27
Gospel	Matthew 18:21-35	Mark 8:27-38	Luke 15:1-10
	Roman Catholic	**Roman Catholic**	**Roman Catholic**
First	Sirach 27:30—28:7	Isaiah 50:5-9a	Exodus 32:7-11, 13-14
Second	Romans 14:7-9	James 2:14-18	1 Timothy 1:12-17
Gospel	Matthew 18:21-35	Mark 8:27-35	Luke 15:1-32

Notes	Special Notes For A	Special Notes For B	Special Notes For C
Creed: Apostles' **Color:** Green **Special Notation:** As soon as Peter declared Jesus to be the Messiah, the veil was lifted for the disciples to see who their Master really was and the path of suffering he would follow.	We need to know and do the work of forgiveness. Our society feels everything is relative and hardly recognizes sin. We must learn ways to say to one another "Your sins are forgiven."	Peter's confession; Jesus' response to deny self and take up his cross and follow.	Consider seeking the lost in our own home.

Music For Worship For Proper 19 — Pentecost 17 — OT 24

NOTES

CYCLE A

Let Me Be Yours Forever
Jesus Sinners Will Receive
Holy Majesty, Before You
Praise To The Father
My Soul, Now Praise Your Maker!
Give To Our God Immortal Praise!
Now Thank We All Our God
Sing Praise To God, The Highest Good
Where Charity And Love Prevail
Praise To The Lord, The Almighty
Praise, My Soul, The King Of Heaven
We Are The Lord's
In Thee Is Gladness

CYCLE B

Let Me Be Yours Forever
Lord Of All Nations, Grant Me Grace
Lord, Whose Love In Humble Service
O God Of Mercy, God Of Light
O Jesus Christ, May Grateful Hymns Be
Rising
Where Cross The Crowded Ways Of Life
The Church Of Christ, In Every Age
By All Your Saints In Warfare
"Take Up Your Cross," The Savior Said
Lord, Thee I Love With All My Heart
Around You, O Lord Jesus

CYCLE C

Forgive Our Sins As We Forgive
Let Me Be Yours Forever
Oh, Sing Jubilee To The Lord
The King Of Love My Shepherd Is
Amazing Grace, How Sweet The Sound

Holy Cross Days
In The Cross Of Christ I Glory
Sing, My Tongue
The Head That Once Was Crowned
Lift High The Cross
When I Survey The Wondrous Cross
Earth And All Stars

Weekly Record

Date			
Entrance Hymn			
Hymn Of The Day			
Anthem / Special Music			
Sermon Title			
Lay Reader			
Attendance			

Proper 20 — Pentecost 18 — OT 25

LESSON	CYCLE A	CYCLE B	CYCLE C
	Revised Common	**Revised Common**	**Revised Common**
First	Exodus 16:2-15	Proverbs 31:10-31	Jeremiah 8:18—9:1
Second	Philippians 1:21-30	James 3:13—4:3, 7-8a	1 Timothy 2:1-7
Gospel	Matthew 20:1-16	Mark 9:30-37	Luke 16:1-13
	Episcopal	**Episcopal**	**Episcopal**
First	Jonah 3:10—4:11	Wisdom 1:16—2:1 (6-11) 12-22	Amos 8:4-7 (8-12)
Second	Philippians 1:21-27	James 3:16—4:6	1 Timothy 2:1-8
Gospel	Matthew 20:1-16	Mark 9:30-37	Luke 16:1-13
	Lutheran	**Lutheran**	**Lutheran**
First	Isaiah 55:6-9	Jeremiah 11:18-20	Amos 8:4-7
Second	Philippians 1:1-5 (6-11) 19-27	James 3:16—4:6	1 Timothy 2:1-8
Gospel	Matthew 20:1-16	Mark 9:30-37	Luke 16:1-13
	Roman Catholic	**Roman Catholic**	**Roman Catholic**
First	Isaiah 55:6-9	Wisdom 2:12, 17-20	Amos 8:4-7
Second	Philippians 1:20c-24, 27	James 3:16—4:3	1 Timothy 2:1-8
Gospel	Matthew 20:1-16	Mark 9:30-37	Luke 16:1-13

Notes	Special Notes For A	Special Notes For B	Special Notes For C
Creed: Apostles' **Color:** Green **Special Notation:** To be number one in God's book is to be a humble disciple and servant of all. Jesus identifies with the hurting and degraded ones.	Work and mission are gifts. They are not to be thought of in terms of hours spent, recognition earned or rewards gained. We live under the curse of the first parents, "by the sweat of your brow you shall eat bread." It is part of the gift of life along with loving others.	The disciples failed to understand what Jesus was teaching. Jesus used a child to illustrate true greatness.	What the steward was doing was giving up his commission, taking the risk that by giving up his share of the money the debtors would receive him into their homes. Jesus takes the same risk in giving up his godliness in order to be received by his people.

Music For Worship For Proper 20 — Pentecost 18 — OT 25

NOTES	CYCLE A	CYCLE B	CYCLE C
	All Depends On Our Possessing Father Eternal, Ruler Of Creation The Son Of God, Our Christ For All Your Saints, O Lord We Are The Lord's All Who Love And Serve Your City Lord Of All Hopefulness	All Depends On Our Possessing A Lamb Goes Uncomplaining Forth Where Charity And Love Prevail Christ Is Alive! Let Christians Sing O God Of Every Nation Children Of The Heavenly Father I Trust, O Christ, In You Alone Lord Christ, When First You Came To Earth	Salvation Unto Us Has Come All Depends On Our Possessing O Trinity, O Blessed Light Your Kingdom Come, O Father Lord, Teach Us How To Pray Aright Son Of God, Eternal Savior Rise Up, O Saints Of God O God Of Every Nation

Weekly Record

Date				
Entrance Hymn				
Hymn Of The Day				
Anthem/ Special Music				
Sermon Title				
Lay Reader				
Attendance				

Proper 21 — Pentecost 19 — OT 26

Readings

LESSON	CYCLE A	CYCLE B	CYCLE C
	Revised Common	**Revised Common**	**Revised Common**
First	Exodus 17:1-7	Esther 7:1-6, 9-10; 9:20-22	Jeremiah 32:1-3a, 6-15
Second	Philippians 2:1-13	James 5:13-20	1 Timothy 6:6-19
Gospel	Matthew 21:23-32	Mark 9:38-50	Luke 16:19-31
	Episcopal	**Episcopal**	**Episcopal**
First	Ezekiel 18:1-4, 25-32	Numbers 11:4-6, 10-16, 24-29	Amos 6:1-7
Second	Philippians 2:1-13	James 4:7-12 (13—5:6)	1 Timothy 6:11-19
Gospel	Matthew 21:28-32	Mark 9:38-43, 45, 47-48	Luke 16:19-31
	Lutheran	**Lutheran**	**Lutheran**
First	Ezekiel 18:1-4, 25-32	Numbers 11:4-6, 10-16, 24-29	Amos 6:1-7
Second	Philippians 2:1-5 (6-11)	James 4:7-12 (13—5:6)	1 Timothy 6:6-16
Gospel	Matthew 21:28-32	Mark 9:38-50	Luke 16:19-31
	Roman Catholic	**Roman Catholic**	**Roman Catholic**
First	Ezekiel 18:25-28	Numbers 11:25-29	Amos 6:1a, 4-7
Second	Philippians 2:1-11	James 5:1-6	1 Timothy 6:11-16
Gospel	Matthew 21:28-32	Mark 8:38-43, 45, 47-48	Luke 16:19-31

Notes	Special Notes For A	Special Notes For B	Special Notes For C
Creed: Apostles' Color: Green Special Notation: Here is a warning against clerical arrogance, triumphalism in the church and a narrow view of God's stability to work in and through all kinds of persons.	The New Testament church and the church of to-day face a common task. While we are told to seek justice, forgive, and be reconcilers in the world, each community must discover its own tasks for its own time.	Theme focuses on all those who do great things for others. Emphasize various agencies with whom the churches share the task of serving and caring for others.	In this parable, Jesus tells the Pharisees, "You are the ones who make yourselves look right in other people's sight, but God knows your hearts. For the things that are considered of great value by man are worth nothing in God's sight."

Music For Worship For Proper 21 — Pentecost 19 — OT 26

NOTES

CYCLE A

Lord, Keep Us Steadfast In Your Word
O Jesus, I Have Promised
Oh, Praise The Lord, My Soul
O Master, Let Me Walk With You

CYCLE B

O Jesus, I Have Promised
Lord, Keep Us Steadfast In Your Word
O Master, Let Me Walk With You
Oh, Praise The Lord, My Soul

CYCLE C

Lord, Keep Us Steadfast In Your Word
O Master, Let Me Walk With You
Oh Jesus, I Have Promised
Praise The Almighty

Weekly Record

Date					
Entrance Hymn					
Hymn Of The Day					
Anthem/ Special Music					
Sermon Title					
Lay Reader					
Attendance					

Proper 22 — Pentecost 20 — OT 27

Readings

LESSON	CYCLE A	CYCLE B	CYCLE C
	Revised Common	**Revised Common**	**Revised Common**
First	Exodus 20:1-4, 7-9, 12-20	Job 1:1—2:1-10	Lamentations 1:1-6
Second	Philippians 3:4b-14	Hebrews 1:1-4; 2:5-12	2 Timothy 1:1-14
Gospel	Matthew 21:33-46	Mark 10:2-16	Luke 17:5-10
	Episcopal	**Episcopal**	**Episcopal**
First	Isaiah 5:1-7	Genesis 2:18-24	Habakkuk 1:1-6 (7-11) 12-13; 2:1-4
Second	Philippians 3:14-21	Hebrews 2:(1-8) 9-18	2 Timothy 1:(1-5) 6-14
Gospel	Matthew 21:33-43	Mark 10:2-9	Luke 17:5-10
	Lutheran	**Lutheran**	**Lutheran**
First	Isaiah 5:1-7	Genesis 2:18-24	Habakkuk 1:1-3; 2:1-14
Second	Philippians 3:12-21	Hebrews 2:9-11 (12-18)	2 Timothy 1:3-14
Gospel	Matthew 21:33-43	Mark 10:2-16	Luke 17:1-10
	Roman Catholic	**Roman Catholic**	**Roman Catholic**
First	Isaiah 5:1-7	Genesis 2:18-24	Habakkuk 1:2-3; 2:2-4
Second	Philippians 4:6-9	Hebrews 2:9-11	2 Timothy 1:6-8, 13-14
Gospel	Matthew 21:33-43	Mark 10:2-16	Luke 17:5-10

Notes

Creed: Apostles'

Color: Green

Special Notation: We must be concerned about God's will, intent and plan. Receptivity and dependence are necessary dispositions for all of God's children.

Special Notes For A

Just as Israel's religious leaders killed the Old Testament prophets, so now they will kill the greatest of them, Jesus, the Messiah. The mission to Israel is abandoned and the gospel is now preached to the gentiles. Sadly, rejection of the gospel is not confined to any age.

Special Notes For B

Theme of marriage and divorce could be emphasized. Jesus uses children as a model of the kingdom.

Special Notes For C

In the middle of the lesson is the cry of the apostles to increase our faith. The only way we can ever hope to respond to the teaching of Christ is by having our faith increased.

Music For Worship For Proper 22 — Pentecost 20 — OT 27

NOTES

CYCLE A

Our Father, By Whose Name
O Jesus, I Have Promised
Come, Gracious Spirit, Heavenly Dove
Breathe On Me Breath Of God
Lord Christ, When First You Come To Earth
Whatever God Ordains Is Right
May God Bestow On Us His Grace

CYCLE B

Look, The Sight Is Glorious
Crown Him With Many Crowns
Cradling Children In His Arm
Oh, Blest The House
For The Beauty Of The Earth

CYCLE C

The Church Of Christ, In Every Age
Our Father, By Whose Name
Out Of The Depths I Cry To You
Lord, Keep Us Steadfast In Your Word
Holy Spirit, Truth Divine
Forgive Our Sins As We Forgive
Eternal Ruler Of The Ceaseless Round

Weekly Record

Date					
Entrance Hymn					
Hymn Of The Day					
Anthem/ Special Music					
Sermon Title					
Lay Reader					
Attendance					

Proper 23 — Pentecost 21 — OT 28

Readings

LESSON	CYCLE A	CYCLE B	CYCLE C
	Revised Common	**Revised Common**	**Revised Common**
First	Exodus 32:1-14	Job 23:1-9, 16-17	Jeremiah 29:1, 4-7
Second	Philippians 4:1-9	Hebrews 4:12-16	2 Timothy 2:8-15
Gospel	Matthew 22:1-14	Mark 10:17-31	Luke 17:11-19
	Episcopal	**Episcopal**	**Episcopal**
First	Isaiah 25:1-9	Amos 5:6-7, 10-15	Ruth 1:(1-7) 8-19a
Second	Philippians 4:4-13	Hebrews 3:1-6	2 Timothy 2:(3-7) 8-15
Gospel	Matthew 22:1-14	Mark 10:17-27 (28-31)	Luke 17:11-19
	Lutheran	**Lutheran**	**Lutheran**
First	Isaiah 25:6-9	Amos 5:6-7, 10-15	Ruth 1:1-19a
Second	Philippians 4:4-13	Hebrews 3:1-6	2 Timothy 2:8-13
Gospel	Matthew 22:1-10 (11-14)	Mark 10:17-27 (28-30)	Luke 17:11-19
	Roman Catholic	**Roman Catholic**	**Roman Catholic**
First	Isaiah 25:6-10	Wisdom 7:7-11	2 Kings 5:14-17
Second	Philippians 4:12-14, 19-20	Hebrews 4:12-13	2 Timothy 2:8-13
Gospel	Matthew 22:1-14	Mark 10:17-30	Luke 17:11-19

Notes

Creed: Apostles'

Color: Green

Special Notation: In following Jesus, persons are challenged to detach themselves from whatever keeps them from giving their total life to him.

Special Notes For A

The Wedding Feast is the New Testament way of speaking of the messianic banquet. The end of all work in the kingdom is the feast. This hope helps us in our work. When we celebrate holy communion, we pray that God would give us a foretaste of the things to come. We partake to be strengthened in our work.

Special Notes For B

How careful we must be not to become hoarders, or prideful owners, or selfish spenders. If our possessions possess us, how can we ever hope to see the treasures of heaven?

Special Notes For C

The season's only miracle story. The theme of foreigners not being foreign in the presence of God, is coupled with faith, thankfulness and healing power.

Music For Worship For Proper 25 — Pentecost 23 — OT 28

NOTES	CYCLE A	CYCLE B	CYCLE C
	All Who Believe And Are Baptized	Thee Will I Love, My Strength	All Who Believe And Are Baptized
	Thee Will I Love, My Strength	Your Hand, O Lord, In Days Of Old	A Multitude Comes From East And West
	Your Hand, O Lord, In Days Of Old	A Multitude Comes From East And West	Thee Will I Love, My Strength
	Son Of God, Eternal Savior	Lord, Save Your World	Once He Came In Blessing
	Around You, O Lord Jesus	O God Of Earth And Altar	Let Us Ever Walk With Jesus
	At The Lamb's High Feast We Sing	Where Restless Crowds Are Thronging	Faith Of Our Fathers
	Who Is This Host Arrayed In White	O Come, Our Help In Ages Past	Jesus, Thy Boundless Love To Me!
	Arise, My Soul, Arise!	"Come, Follow Me," The Savior Spake	Give To Our God Immortal Praise!
	The Lord's My Shepherd	Let Me Be Yours Forever	Sing Praise To God, The Highest Good
	The King Of Love My Shepherd Is	Hope Of The World	Rejoice, O Pilgrim Throng!
	Jesus! The Boundless Love To Me		
	Rejoice, The Lord Is King!		

Weekly Record

Date					
Entrance Hymn					
Hymn Of The Day					
Anthem/ Special Music					
Sermon Title					
Lay Reader					
Attendance					

Proper 24 — Pentecost 22 — OT 29

Readings

LESSON		CYCLE A	CYCLE B	CYCLE C
		Revised Common	**Revised Common**	**Revised Common**
First		Exodus 33:12-23	Job 38:1-7 (34-41)	Jeremiah 31:27-34
Second		1 Thessalonians 1:1-10	Hebrews 5:1-10	2 Timothy 3:14—4:5
Gospel		Matthew 22:15-22	Mark 10:35-45	Luke 18:1-8
		Episcopal	**Episcopal**	**Episcopal**
First		Isaiah 45:1-7	Isaiah 53:4-12	Genesis 32:3-8, 22-30
Second		1 Thessalonians 1:1-10	Hebrews 4:12-16	2 Timothy 3:14—4:5
Gospel		Matthew 22:15-21	Mark 10:35-45	Luke 18:1-8a
		Lutheran	**Lutheran**	**Lutheran**
First		Isaiah 45:1-7	Isaiah 53:10-12	Genesis 32:22-30
Second		1 Thessalonians 1:1-5a	Hebrews 4:9-16	2 Timothy 3:14—4:5
Gospel		Matthew 22:15-21	Mark 10:34-45	Luke 18:1-8a
		Roman Catholic	**Roman Catholic**	**Roman Catholic**
First		Isaiah 45:1, 4-6	Isaiah 53:10-11	Exodus 17:8-13
Second		1 Thessalonians 1:1-5a	Hebrews 4:14-16	2 Timothy 3:14—4:2
Gospel		Matthew 22:15-21	Mark 10:35-45	Luke 18:1-8

Notes

Notes	Special Notes For A	Special Notes For B	Special Notes For C
Creed: Apostles' **Color:** Green **Special Notation:** God reminded the disciples that his radical new way was not to transform the world from top down.	Rendering to Caesar or to God.	Theme is connected with discipleship. "Whoever would be great among you must be your servant." Emphasize various ways members could and do carry out their ministry in the work-a-day world. Use vocations, avocations, in-church service, community projects, neighborly and friendly outreach, educational and artistic talents, youth and elderly involvement and prison work.	It is easy to lose heart at times. We often feel God doesn't care about us. But the gospel ends the same way Jacob's wrestling match ended — with the very promise of blessing.

Music For Worship For Proper 24 — Pentecost 22 — OT 29

NOTES

CYCLE A	CYCLE B	CYCLE C
Forth In Thy Name, O Lord I Go	God, Who Stretched The Spangled Heavens	Forth In Thy Name, O Lord, I Go
God, Who Stretched The Spangled Heavens	Out Of The Depths, I Cry To You	Father Eternal Ruler Of Creation
Out Of The Depths I Cry To You	Father Eternal Ruler Of Creation	God, Who Stretched The Spangled Heavens
Father Eternal Ruler Of Creation	O Christ, Our Hope	Unto The Hills
Earth And All Stars!	Love Consecrates The Humblest Act	
Eternal Ruler Of The Ceaseless Round	The Son Of God Goes Forth To War	
Come Holy Ghost, Our Souls Inspire	Lord, Whose Love In Humble Service	
Lord Of Glory, You Have Bought Us	O Master, Let Me Walk With You	

Weekly Record

Date			
Entrance Hymn			
Hymn Of The Day			
Anthem/ Special Music			
Sermon Title			
Lay Reader			
Attendance			

Reformation Sunday

Readings

LESSON	CYCLE A	CYCLE B	CYCLE C
First Second Gospel	Revised Common	Revised Common	Revised Common
First Second Gospel	Episcopal	Episcopal	Episcopal
First Second Gospel	Lutheran Jeremiah 31:31-34 Romans 3:19-28 John 8:31-36	Lutheran Jeremiah 31:31-34 Romans 3:19-28 John 8:31-36	Lutheran Jeremiah 31:31-34 Romans 3:19-28 John 8:31-36
First Second Gospel	Roman Catholic	Roman Catholic	Roman Catholic

Notes	Special Notes For A	Special Notes For B	Special Notes For C
Creed: Apostles' Color: Red Special Notation: God's people can celebrate this new exodus experience in Christ as it frees them from all that tries to shackle and turn them in upon themselves.	This festival could replace the 20th Sunday after Pentecost or be held during the week. If held on Sunday, the chorale service of holy communion might be a good choice. Procession is appropriate.	All have sinned, so Christ died for all. He rose from death, hear his love call. God justified sinners through grace; Saved by the faith, no matter their race.	Luther's Seal Banner could be processed. Appropriate time to use chorale service of holy communion LBW, p. 120.

Music For Worship For Reformation Sunday

NOTES

CYCLE A	CYCLE B	CYCLE C
A Mighty Fortress Is Our God God's Word Is Our Great Heritage Lord, Keep Us Steadfast In Your Word O God, O Lord Of Heaven And Earth The Church's One Foundation	A Mighty Fortress Is Our God God's Word Is Our Great Heritage Lord, Keep Us Steadfast In Your Word O God, O Lord Of Heaven And Earth The Church's One Foundation	A Mighty Fortress Is Our God Lord, Keep Us Steadfast In Your Word God's Word Is Our Great Heritage Salvation Unto Us Has Come The Church's One Foundation O God, O Lord Of Heaven And Earth Faith Of Our Fathers

Weekly Record

Date			
Entrance Hymn			
Hymn Of The Day			
Anthem/ Special Music			
Sermon Title			
Lay Reader			
Attendance			

All Saints' Day

Readings

LESSON	CYCLE A	CYCLE B	CYCLE C
	Revised Common	**Revised Common**	**Revised Common**
First	Revelation 7:9-17	Wisdom of Solomon 3:1-9	Daniel 7:1-3, 15-18
Second	1 John 3:1-3	Revelation 21:1-6a	Ephesians 1:11-23
Gospel	Matthew 5:1-12	John 11:32-44	Luke 6:20-31
	Episcopal	**Episcopal**	**Episcopal**
First	Ecclesiasticus 44:1-10, 13-14	Ecclesiasticus 44:1-10, 13-14	Ecclesiasticus 44:1-10, 13-14
Second	Revelation 7:2-4, 9-17	Revelation 7:2-4, 9-17	Revelation 7:2-4, 9-12
Gospel	Matthew 5:1-12	Matthew 5:1-12	Matthew 5:1-12
	Lutheran	**Lutheran**	**Lutheran**
First	Isaiah 26:1-4, 8-9, 12-13, 19-21	Isaiah 26:1-4, 8-9, 12-13, 19-21	Isaiah 26:1-4, 8-9, 12-13, 19-21
Second	Revelation 21:9-11, 22-27 (22:1-5)	Revelation 21:9-11, 22-27 (22:1-5)	Revelation 21:9-11, 22-27 (22:1-5)
Gospel	Matthew 5:1-12	Matthew 5:1-12	Matthew 5:1-12
	Roman Catholic	**Roman Catholic**	**Roman Catholic**
First	Revelation 7:2-4, 9-12	Revelation 7:2-4, 9-12	Revelation 7:2-4, 9-12
Second	1 John 3:1-3	1 John 3:1-3	1 John 3:1-3
Gospel	Matthew 5:1-12	Matthew 5:1-12	Matthew 5:1-12

Notes

Creed: Apostles'
Color: White
Special Notation: Appropriate occasion for baptisms.

Special Notes For A

Now we face death. We are called to carry out the mission of the church in good and in hard times, always remembering that others have gone before us. Christ has been followed by others known and unknown to us. They found grace sufficient to sustain them and the hope of salvation sufficient to encourage them. Those who have died during the past year can be named.

Special Notes For B

Grace is the theme. Theology of Beatitudes appears in today's gospel. The blessedness of those who rest wholly on the mercy of God is seen in this passage. Whatever our moods of skepticism and depression, Christ and his victory over death and the grave stand impregnable and secure.

Special Notes For C

Might use loaf of bread in place of wafers. Also might stand to recognize all saints and name those who died in past year.

Music For Worship For All Saints' Day

NOTES	CYCLE A	CYCLE B	CYCLE C
	For All The Saints For All Your Saints, O Lord Oh, What Their Joy Who Is This Host Arrayed In White	For All The Saints For All Your Saints, O Lord Oh, What Their Joy Who Is This Host Arrayed In White	For All The Saints For All Your Saints, O Lord By All Your Saints In Warfare Come, Risen Lord Draw Near And Take The Body Of The Lord Who Is This Host O God, Our Help In Ages Past Oh, What Their Joy The Church's One Foundation

Weekly Record

Date			
Entrance Hymn			
Hymn Of The Day			
Anthem/ Special Music			
Sermon Title			
Lay Reader			
Attendance			

Proper 25 — Pentecost 23 — OT 30

Readings

LESSON	CYCLE A	CYCLE B	CYCLE C
	Revised Common	**Revised Common**	**Revised Common**
First	Deuteronomy 34:1-12	Job 42:1-6, 10-17	Joel 2:23-32
Second	1 Thessalonians 2:1-8	Hebrews 7:23-28	2 Timothy 4:6-8, 16-18
Gospel	Matthew 22:34-46	Mark 10:46-52	Luke 18:9-14
	Episcopal	**Episcopal**	**Episcopal**
First	Exodus 22:21-27	Isaiah 59:(1-4) 9-19	Jeremiah 14:(1-6) 7-10, 19-22
Second	1 Thessalonians 2:1-8	Hebrews 5:12—6:1, 9-12	2 Timothy 4:6-8, 16-18
Gospel	Matthew 22:34-46	Mark 10:46-52	Luke 18:9-14
	Lutheran	**Lutheran**	**Lutheran**
First	Leviticus 9:1-2, 15-18	Jeremiah 31:7-9	Deuteronomy 10:12-22
Second	1 Thessalonians 1:5b-10	Hebrews 5:1-10	2 Timothy 4:6-8, 16-18
Gospel	Matthew 22:34-40 (41-46)	Mark 10:46-52	Luke 18:9-14
	Roman Catholic	**Roman Catholic**	**Roman Catholic**
First	Exodus 22:20-27	Jeremiah 31:7-9	Sirach 35:12c-14, 16-18b
Second	1 Thessalonians 1:5-10	Hebrews 5:1-6	2 Timothy 4:6-8, 16-18
Gospel	Matthew 22:34-40	Mark 10:46-52	Luke 18:9-14

Notes

Creed: Apostles'
Color: Green
Special Notation: Theme: Loving God and others *as* we love ourselves.

Special Notes For A

The lessons speak of how the faithful are to live as they await the banquet. Jesus says the greatest commandment (to love God) is like the second (to love one another). No person can do one without doing the other.

Special Notes For B

The blind beggar threw aside his most important possession (his cloak) and ran to reach the one in whom he had placed his trust. This is "Faith for the road." It should propel us into the thick of life and the joy of exhausting servanthood on "the Way." A blind person may be invited to read the gospel. Also a handicapped person could pray the prayers.

Special Notes For C

Every tower of Babel we construct eventually crashes to dust. But those whom God raises up are raised forever. That is why Jesus kicked down the egotistic towers of the Pharisees, so that rather than having to stand on their own shaky foundation, they too might be held in the hands of God, like the publican who knew that his only security was in the mercy of God.

NOTES

CYCLE A	CYCLE B	CYCLE C
Lord, Teach Us How To Pray Aright Oh, Praise The Lord, My Soul To You, Omniscient Lord Of All Rise Up, O Saints Of God! Your Word, O Lord, Is Gentle Dew God Of Our Life, All Glorious Lord Lord, Thee I Love With All My Heart Jesus, Thy Boundless Love To Me Spirit Of God, Descend Upon My Heart O God, I Love Thee Hope Of The World Jesus Calls Us; O'er The Tumult Thee Will I Love, My Strength O Jesus, King Most Wonderful!	O Praise The Lord, My Soul To You, Omniscient Lord Of All Oh, That The Lord Would Guide My Ways O Son Of God, In Galilee Your Hand, O Lord, In Days Of Old O God, Whose Will Is Love And Good Amazing Grace, How Sweet The Sound God, Whose Almighty Word Sing Praise To God, The Highest Good	Lord, Teach Us How To Pray Aright Oh, That The Lord Would Guide My Ways Oh, Praise The Lord, My Soul

Weekly Record

Date				
Entrance Hymn				
Hymn Of The Day				
Anthem/ Special Music				
Sermon Title				
Lay Reader				
Attendance				

Proper 26 — Pentecost 24 — OT 31

Readings

LESSON		CYCLE A	CYCLE B	CYCLE C
		Revised Common	**Revised Common**	**Revised Common**
First		Joshua 3:7-17	Ruth 1:1-18	Habakkuk 1:1-4; 2:1-4
Second		1 Thessalonians 2:9-13	Hebrews 9:11-14	2 Thessalonians 1:1-4, 11-12
Gospel		Matthew 23:1-12	Mark 12:28-34	Luke 19:1-10
		Episcopal	**Episcopal**	**Episcopal**
First		Micah 3:5-12	Deuteronomy 6:1-9	Isaiah 1:10-20
Second		1 Thessalonians 2:9-13, 17-20	Hebrews 7:23-28	2 Thessalonians 1:1-5 (6-10) 11-12
Gospel		Matthew 23:1-12	Mark 12:28-34	Luke 19:1-10
		Lutheran	**Lutheran**	**Lutheran**
First		Amos 5:18-24	Deuteronomy 6:1-9	Exodus 34:5-9
Second		1 Thessalonians 4:13-14 (15-18)	Hebrews 7:23-28	2 Thessalonians 1:1-5, 11-12
Gospel		Matthew 25:1-13	Mark 12:28-34 (35-37)	Luke 19:1-10
		Roman Catholic	**Roman Catholic**	**Roman Catholic**
First		Malachi 1:14a—2:2b, 8-10	Deuteronomy 6:2-6	Wisdom 11:22—12:1
Second		1 Thessalonians 2:7-9, 13	Hebrews 7:23-28	2 Thessalonians 1:11—2:2
Gospel		Matthew 23:1-12	Mark 12:28-34	Luke 19:1-10

Notes	Special Notes For A	Special Notes For B	Special Notes For C
Creed: Apostles' **Color:** Green **Special Notation:** In mission outreach our service to others should display its source in our love of God.	Theme: The least and the greatest.	Theme is total love of God and neighbor. Jesus puts them together. They flow from and into the other. Emphasize outreach and mission.	The difference in the "before" and "after" pictures of Zacchaeus indicates that what Jesus brought to him was rebirth, salvation, a place in the family for one who had been an outcast. Children could sing "Zacchaeus was a wee little man."

NOTES

CYCLE A	CYCLE B	CYCLE C
Love Divine, All Loves Excelling Lord Of Light If You But Trust In God To Guide You The Lord Will Come And Not Be Slow I Know Of A Sleep In Jesus' Name Oh, Happy Day When We Shall Stand Rejoice, Rejoice, Believers Soul, Adorn Yourself With Gladness	Lord Of Light If You But Trust In God To Guide You Wake, Awake, Night Is Flying Oh, That The Lord Would Guide My Ways My God, How Wonderful Thou Art I Know That My Redeemer Lives! God Of Our Life, All-Glorious Lord Lord, Thee I Love With All My Heart O God I Love Thee Hope Of The World Jesus Calls Us, O'er The Tumult Thee Will I Love, My Strength O Jesus, King Most Wonderful	Lord Divine, All Loves Excelling Wake, Awake, For Night Is Flying Lord Of Light If You But Trust In God To Guide You Before You, Lord, We Bow All Creatures Of Our God And King Jesus Sinners Will Receive One There Is, Above All Others Today Your Mercy Calls Us Chief Of Sinners Though I Be

Weekly Record

Date			
Entrance Hymn			
Hymn Of The Day			
Anthem/ Special Music			
Sermon Title			
Lay Reader			
Attendance			

Proper 27 — Pentecost 25 — OT 32

Proper 27 — Pentecost 25 — OT 32

Readings

LESSON		CYCLE A	CYCLE B	CYCLE C
		Revised Common	**Revised Common**	**Revised Common**
First		Joshua 24:1-3a, 14-25	Ruth 3:1-5; 4:13-17	Haggai 1:15b—2:9
Second		1 Thessalonians 4:13-18	Hebrews 9:24-28	2 Thessalonians 2:1-5, 13-17
Gospel		Matthew 25:1-13	Mark 12:38-44	Luke 20:27-38
		Episcopal	**Episcopal**	**Episcopal**
First		Amos 5:18-24	1 Kings 17:8-16	Job 19:23-27a
Second		1 Thessalonians 4:13-18	Hebrews 9:24-28	2 Thessalonians 2:13—3:5
Gospel		Matthew 25:1-13	Mark 12:38-44	Luke 20:27-38
		Lutheran	**Lutheran**	**Lutheran**
First		Hosea 11:1-4, 8-9	1 Kings 17:8-16	1 Chronicles 29:10-13
Second		1 Thessalonians 5:1-11	Hebrews 9:24-28	2 Thessalonians 2:13—3:5
Gospel		Matthew 25:14-30	Mark 12:41-44	Luke 20:27-38
		Roman Catholic	**Roman Catholic**	**Roman Catholic**
First		Wisdom 6:12-16	1 Kings 17:8-16	2 Maccabees 7:1-2, 9-14
Second		1 Thessalonians 4:13-14 (15-18)	Hebrews 9:24-28	2 Thessalonians 2:16—3:5
Gospel		Matthew 25:1-13	Mark 12:38-44	Luke 20:27-38

Notes	Special Notes For A	Special Notes For B	Special Notes For C
Creed: Apostles' **Color:** Green **Special Notation:** Our giving should be the result of trust in and commitment to God.	Themes are wise and foolish maidens.	The widow's mite: the term should inspire complete loyalty and devotion to God's call. The dialog between Elijah and the widow could be read by a narrator and 2 other people.	Faithfulness to God does not mean devising trick questions based upon his law. It means being open to the new life he promises to bring.

Music For Worship For Proper 27 — Pentecost 25 — OT 32

NOTES

CYCLE A

Rejoice, Angelic Choirs, Rejoice!
As Saints Of Old
I Know That My Redeemer Lives!
O God, Our Help In Ages Past
Praise To The Lord, The Almighty
We Are The Lord's
Raise, My Soul, To Watch And Pray
Lord Of Light
God, Whose Giving Knows No Ending

CYCLE B

As Saints Of Old
I Know That My Redeemer Lives!
Forth In Thy Name, O Lord, I Go
Lord, Our God, With Praise We Come
Take My Life, That I May Be

CYCLE C

Rejoice, Angelic Choirs, Rejoice!
Forth In Thy Name, O Lord, I Go
As Saints Of Old
Praise The Lord, O Heavens

Weekly Record

Date			
Entrance Hymn			
Hymn Of The Day			
Anthem/ Special Music			
Sermon Title			
Lay Reader			
Attendance			

LESSON

CYCLE A

Revised Common
First — Judges 4:1-7
Second — 1 Thessalonians 5:1-11
Gospel — Matthew 25:14-30

Episcopal
First — Zephaniah 1:7, 12-18
Second — 1 Thessalonians 5:1-10
Gospel — Matthew 25:14-15, 19-29

Lutheran
First — Malachi 2:1-2, 4-10
Second — 1 Thessalonians 2:8-13
Gospel — Matthew 23:1-12

Roman Catholic
First — Proverbs 31:10-13, 19-20, 30-31
Second — 1 Thessalonians 5:1-6
Gospel — Matthew 25:14-15 (16-30)

CYCLE B

Revised Common
First — 1 Samuel 1:4-20
Second — Hebrews 10:11-14, (15-18)
Gospel — Mark 13:1-8

Episcopal
First — Daniel 12.1-4a (5-13)
Second — Hebrews 10:31-39
Gospel — Mark 13:14-23

Lutheran
First — Daniel 12:1-3
Second — Hebrews 10:11-18
Gospel — Mark 13:1-13

Roman Catholic
First — Daniel 12:1-3
Second — Hebrews 10:11-14, 18
Gospel — Mark 13:24-32

CYCLE C

Revised Common
First — Isaiah 65:17-25
Second — 2 Thessalonians 3:6-13
Gospel — Luke 21:5-19

Episcopal
First — Malachi 3:13—4:2a, 5-6
Second — 2 Thessalonians 3:6-13
Gospel — Luke 21:5-19

Lutheran
First — Malachi 4:1-2a
Second — 2 Thessalonians 3:6-13
Gospel — Luke 21:5-19

Roman Catholic
First — Malachi 3:19-20 (4:1-2)
Second — 2 Thessalonians 3:7-12
Gospel — Luke 21:5-19

Notes

Creed: Apostles'
Color: Green
Special Notation: "Take Heed." (Theme of endtime). Be faithful witnesses before false prophets, tempting individuals and dark forces.

Special Notes For A

Servants and masters and the use of our talents is the theme.

Special Notes For B

Theme: The destruction of Jerusalem; nation against nation; gospel to the whole world; messianic coming.

Special Notes For C

As the once healthy and beautiful leaves of summer now are crushed underfoot, so it is with the entire creation of humanity and all of creation. It shall end in dust and decay. Any eternal security for humanity is found only in God.

Music For Worship For Proper 28 — Pentecost 26 — OT 33

NOTES

CYCLE A	CYCLE B	CYCLE C
Through The Night Of Doubt And Sorrow	Through The Night Of Doubt And Sorrow	O God Of Earth And Altar
Fight The Good Fight	Oh That The Lord Would Guide My Ways	Through The Night Of Doubt And Sorrow
The Lord Will Come And Not Be Slow	When All Your Mercies, O My God	Earth And Stars!
The Day Is Surely Drawing Near	Forth In Thy Name, O Lord, I Go	Christ, Whose Glory Fills The Skies
The Clouds Of Judgment Gather	O Christ, Our Hope	Judge Eternal, Throned In Splendor
O Lord Of Light, Who Made The Stars	Jesus, Your Blood And Righteousness	All Creatures Of Our God And King
Rise, My Soul, To Watch And Pray	Lord, Keep Us Steadfast In Your Word	This Is My Father's World
Lead On, O King Eternal	Lord Christ, When First You Come To Earth	
Lord Our God, With Praise We Come	Come, Oh, Come, O Quickening Spirit	
Dear Lord And Father Of Mankind		
Come Down, O Love Divine		
God, Whose Giving Knows No Ending		
God The Father, Be Our Stay		
Lord Jesus, Think On Me		

Weekly Record

Date		
Entrance Hymn		
Hymn Of The Day		
Anthem/ Special Music		
Sermon Title		
Lay Reader		
Attendance		

Readings

LESSON	CYCLE A	CYCLE B	CYCLE C
	Revised Common	Revised Common	Revised Common
First			
Second			
Gospel			
	Episcopal	Episcopal	Episcopal
First			
Second			
Gospel			
	Lutheran	Lutheran	Lutheran
First	Jeremiah 26:1-6	Daniel 7:9-10	Isaiah 52:1-6
Second	1 Thessalonians 3:7-13	Hebrews 13:20-21	1 Corinthians 15:54-58
Gospel	Matthew 24:1-14	Mark 13:24-31	Luke 19:11-27
	Roman Catholic	Roman Catholic	Roman Catholic
First			
Second			
Gospel			

Notes	Special Notes For A	Special Notes For B	Special Notes For C
Creed: Apostles' **Color:** Green **Special Notation:** The God who will reign majestic above all and who will call us to judgment is the same God who meets us in Jesus.	This presents a call to godliness and a concern that all believers urge their brethren to abound in love to all people. The children should be encouraged to enact, or portray by picture or story, some decisions of right over wrong whereby they stand fast in the Lord.	Great changes will take place in the world when the Son of Man comes again. Great sorrowing and tribulations will precede the judgment. The second lesson is a short prayer by Paul for the Hebrews. The first lesson is a vision of God on his throne with the multitude before him and the great books open.	We are told three things: The end is coming, the end is not yet, until it comes we have dominion (Genesis). All of us ought to be concerned.

Music For Worship For Pentecost 27

NOTES

CYCLE A	CYCLE B	CYCLE C
The Day Is Surely Drawing Near Rejoice, Rejoice Believers Lord Christ, When First You Came To Earth Lo! He Comes With Clouds Descending The Lord Will Come And Not Be Slow The Clouds Of Judgment Gather O Lord Of Light Who Made The Stars Rise, My Soul, To Watch And Pray Rise, O Children Of Salvation Herald, Sound The Note Of Judgment My Hope Is Built On Nothing Less	Rejoice, Rejoice, Believers The Day Is Surely Drawing Near Jerusalem, My Happy Home Guide Me Ever, Great Redeemer	The Day Is Surely Drawing Near Rise, O Children Of Salvation Rejoice, Rejoice, Believers Wake, Awake, For Night Is Flying Jerusalem, My Happy Home Jerusalem, The Golden With High Delight Let Us Unite Make Songs Of Joy Christ Jesus Lay In Death's Strong Bands

Weekly Record

Date				
Entrance Hymn				
Hymn Of The Day				
Anthem/ Special Music				
Sermon Title				
Lay Reader				
Attendance				

Christ The King Sunday

Readings

LESSON		CYCLE A	CYCLE B	CYCLE C
		Revised Common	**Revised Common**	**Revised Common**
First		Ezekiel 34:11-16, 20-24	2 Samuel 23:1-7	Jeremiah 23:1-6
Second		Ephesians 1:15-23	Revelation 1:4b-8	Colossians 1:11-20
Gospel		Matthew 25:31-46	John 18:33-37	Luke 23:33-43
		Episcopal	**Episcopal**	**Episcopal**
First		Ezekiel 24:11-17	Daniel 7:9-14	Jeremiah 23:1-6
Second		1 Corinthians 15:20-28	Revelation 1:1-8	Colossians 1:11-20
Gospel		Matthew 25:31-46	John 18:33-37	Luke 23:35-43
		Lutheran	**Lutheran**	**Lutheran**
First		Ezekiel 34:11-16, 23-24	Daniel 7:13-14	Jeremiah 23:2-6
Second		1 Corinthians 15:20-28	Revelation 1:4b-8	Colossians 1:13-20
Gospel		Matthew 25:31-46	John 18:33-37	Luke 23:35-43 or Luke 19:29-38
		Roman Catholic	**Roman Catholic**	**Roman Catholic**
First		Ezekiel 34:11-12, 15-17	Daniel 7:13-14	2 Samuel 5:1-3
Second		1 Corinthians 15:20-26, 28	Revelation 1:5-8	Colossians 1:12-20
Gospel		Matthew 25:31-46	John 18:33-37	Luke 23:35-43

Notes	Special Notes For A	Special Notes For B	Special Notes For C
Creed: Apostles' **Color:** White **Special Notation:** Basis for the last judgment.	This Sunday speaks of that end of the age when the kingdom comes to full flower. All of the gifts of the earth finally are brought to the Lamb and healing comes to all.	The tiny, persecuted band of Christians who received the book of Revelation clung to the hope that our Lord will reign over all nations and put his enemies under his feet. Christ who continued to serve these Christians will rule over all earthly rulers. We, too, know that because he is king, we belong to royalty. The dialog between Pilate and Jesus could be read by a narrator and two other people.	This story seems to belong to Holy Week. But it tells us exactly what the kingdom of the King is all about. It's about death at the hands of the world, but it's also about power of which the world can only dream — power over death. We are part of that kingdom.

Music For Worship For Christ The King Sunday

NOTES

CYCLE A	CYCLE B	CYCLE C
Rejoice The Lord Is King!	Rejoice, The Lord Is King!	Rejoice, The Lord Is King!
At The Name Of Jesus	The Head That Once Was Crowned	The Day Is Surely Drawing Near
O Jesus, King Most Wonderful!	All Hail The Power Of Jesus' Name!	At The Name Of Jesus
The Head That Once Was Crowned		The Heat That Once Was Crowned
Crown Him With Many Crowns	Christ Is Alive! Let Christians Sing	
Lord, Enthroned In Heavenly Splendor	Christ Is The King!	All Hail The Power Of Jesus' Name!
All Hail The Power Of Jesus' Name!	Jesus Shall Reign	Christ Is Alive! Let Christians Sing
Christ Is Alive! Let Christians Sing	The King Shall Come	Christ Is The King!
Christ Is The King!		Jesus Shall Reign
Jesus Shall Reign		The King Shall Come
The King Shall Come		

Weekly Record

Date					
Entrance Hymn					
Hymn Of The Day					
Anthem/ Special Music					
Sermon Title					
Lay Reader					
Attendance					

Thanksgiving Day

Readings

LESSON	CYCLE A	CYCLE B	CYCLE C
First Second Gospel	**Revised Common** Deuteronomy 8:7-18 2 Corinthians 9:6-15 Luke 7:11-19	**Revised Common** Joel 2:21-27 1 Timothy 2:1-7 Matthew 6:25-33	**Revised Common** Deuteronomy 26:1-11 Philippians 4:4-9 John 6:25-35
First Second Gospel	**Episcopal** Deuteronomy 8:1-3, 6-10 James 1:17-18, 21-27 Matthew 6:25-33	**Episcopal** Deuteronomy 8:1-3, 6-10 James 1:17-18, 21-27 Matthew 6:25-33	**Episcopal** Deuteronomy 8:1-3, 6-10 James 1:17-18, 21-27 Matthew 6:25-33
First Second Gospel	**Lutheran** Deuteronomy 8:1-10 Philippians 4:6-20 Luke 17:11-19	**Lutheran** Deuteronomy 8:1-10 Philippians 4:6-20 Luke 17:11-19	**Lutheran** Deuteronomy 8:1-10 Philippians 4:6-20 Luke 17:11-19
First Second Gospel	**Roman Catholic**	**Roman Catholic**	**Roman Catholic**

Notes	Special Notes For A	Special Notes For B	Special Notes For C
Creed: Apostles' **Color:** White **Special Notation:** Remember the blessings of land, air and water. Christians remember with thanksgiving the God of the First Article of the Apostles' Creed.	A time of thanks for the gifts of life and property. This festival can be used as a time of sharing. The offertory celebrates our whole life as a gift to be lived with zest and to be shared with others. Church agencies can provide information for understanding justice issues that Christians face today.	We are told to be thankful for all people, as God wants everyone to be saved. As Christians let us not miss opportunities to praise God for daily blessings, great or small.	Invite members to write down things for which they are thankful. Remind them especially of ordinary things taken for granted and burdens which help us grow. A search will uncover a list longer than ever imagined. Those who wish might share a specific thanksgiving at the service.

Music For Worship For Thanksgiving Day

NOTES

CYCLE A	CYCLE B	CYCLE C
Come, You Thankful People, Come For The Fruit Of All Creation Let All Things Now Living Now Thank We All Our God Praise And Thanksgiving Sing To The Lord Of Harvest We Praise You, O God When All Your Mercies, O My God	Come, You Thankful People, Come For The Fruit Of All Creation Let All Things Now Living Now Thank We All Our God Praise And Thanksgiving Sing To The Lord Of Harvest We Praise You, O God When All Your Mercies, O My God	Come, You Thankful People, Come Let All Things Now Living Now Thank We All Our God Praise And Thanksgiving Sing To The Lord Of Harvest We Praise You, O God When All Your Mercies, O My God

Weekly Record

Date					
Entrance Hymn					
Hymn Of The Day					
Anthem/ Special Music					
Sermon Title					
Lay Reader					
Attendance					

You may copy pages 148-149 for special situations

Readings

LESSON	CYCLE A	CYCLE B	CYCLE C
First Second Gospel			
First Second Gospel			
First Second Gospel			
First Second Gospel			
Notes	Special Notes For A	Special Notes For B	Special Notes For C

Creed:
Color:
Special Notation:

Music For Worship

NOTES	CYCLE A	CYCLE B	CYCLE C

Weekly Record

Date					
Entrance Hymn					
Hymn Of The Day					
Anthem/ Special Music					
Sermon Title					
Lay Reader					
Attendance